Praise for *Freeing Celibacy:*

"Many have questioned whether there is sufficient connection between priesthood and celibacy to warrant the Roman Rite requirement that only celibates be ordained. Few, however, have argued as cogently as Donald Cozzens for that requirement to be abandoned.

As a Bishop from Oceania, a region where the requirement of celibacy for ordination leads to a continued dearth of priests for evangelization, pastoral care, and regular celebration of the Mass, I am deeply grateful to Donald Cozzens for setting out so compellingly the arguments for an urgent review of the present discipline in the Roman Rite.

Pastoral bishops arguing for a reconsideration of the present insistence that Roman Rite priests be celibates will be both helped and heartened by Donald Cozzens's admirable review of the ecclesial and pastoral value of mandatory celibacy."

Cardinal Thomas Williams
Archbishop of Wellington
New Zealand

"With his trademark clarity, insight, and wisdom, Donald Cozzens has written the best book on the controversial topic of celibacy in many years. Certainly one of the most misunderstood practices of the Christian tradition, celibacy has been both wrongly elevated over the married life, and unfairly blamed for the sexual abuse scandals. Cozzens's superb new book places celibacy in its proper historical and theological context and, in the process, shows how the healthy celibate can be not only productive, but also holy."

James Martin, S.J.
Author of *My Life with the Saints*

"Fr. Donald Cozzens, a respected priest, teacher, seminary rector, and author, argues persuasively that the charism of celibacy as a gift of the Spirit should be distinguished and released from the canonical mandate of celibacy as a condition for ordination to the priesthood. While recognizing the great contribution of priests gifted with the charism of celibacy to the Church, he empathizes with the priests, who strive by the grace of God to live the celibate life without being blessed with the charism of celibacy. He concludes, 'the time has come to set celibacy free.'"

Bishop Joseph M. Sullivan
(Ret.) Auxiliary Bishop
Diocese of Brooklyn

"*Freeing Celibacy* is one of the clearest and most straightforward examinations of the role of obligatory celibacy in the Roman Catholic priesthood and in the life of the Church. In his characteristically low-key, even gentle fashion, Father Cozzens effectively challenges each of the traditional defenses that have been mounted in support of the discipline. The book, in effect, points its finger at a massive elephant in the Church's living room that many still pretend not to see."

Richard P. McBrien
University of Notre Dame

"Combining history, theology, pastoral experience, and sincere love for the church, *Freeing Celibacy* is a courageous, forward-looking book that invites reflection and discussion on the role of celibacy in the life of the church. Donald Cozzens, in the clear, readable style that has distinguished his earlier writings on the priesthood, challenges the church to see celibacy in the only way that fully describes its proper meaning, namely, as a gracious gift of God freely chosen and freely lived. A must-read for all who are concerned about the continued viability of eucharistic communities."

William H. Shannon
Nazareth College
Rochester, New York

"*Freeing Celibacy,* what a marvelous double entendre! With wisdom, compassions, and passion Cozzens argues that celibacy for the diocesan clergy is 'freeing'—an experience of freedom and joy—only if the church 'frees' it from legalism, fear of sexuality, and lust for power, that is, only if we have the courage to let it be what it essentially is—a gift/charism from God. This book must be meditated upon by every bishop, priest, candidate to the priesthood, and by anyone concerned about the future of the Roman Catholic Church."

Peter C. Phan, Ph.D.
Theology Department
Georgetown University

Father Cozzens, in his usual insightful way, has given us a fresh way to look at priestly celibacy. One finishes the book with a resounding 'why not?' to the issue of optional celibacy. Only a priest with his rich and varied background, as well as his understanding of celibacy through faithful service to the Church, has the authority and wisdom to write what will be the authoritative book on the subject.

Paul Wilkes
Author of *In Mysterious Ways: The Death and Life of a Parish Priest*

"Here is what we need to know about the relatively short history of mandatory celibacy for diocesan priests, about its nature, its giftedness, and its difficulty. Cozzens writes with directness, honesty, and respect—for celibacy, for those who attempt it, and for those who will not free it for the good of all God's people. And we don't need to be ordained priests to appreciate what he says and to see celibacy in a new light. This is such a fine book!"

Stefanie Weisgram, O.S.B.
Former book review editor, *Sisters Today*

"Using part of the title of his last book, we can definitely say that Donald Cozzens 'dares to speak'—and thank God for him and his commitment to the truth. In *Freeing Celibacy* he explores the theology, history, and sociology of both mandated and charismatic clerical celibacy. He looks at the reality of church governance and listens to the testimony of priests and laity. He recognizes and lauds the power and grace of the genuine charism of priestly celibacy, but celibacy merely mandated yields unnecessary problems and horrors for him. He amasses his evidence in such a compelling way that even the hierarchs may hear him: Mandated celibacy is ready for repeal!"

Andrew P. Connolly
Saint Francis de Sales Parish
Patchogue, New York

"Father Cozzens is correct in saying that the issue of priestly celibacy needs a full and open discussion. There is too much secrecy and misinformation about the priesthood today, and Cozzens helps by opening up the windows. Cozzens speaks from decades of experience, giving him judgment about the gifts and limitations of men in the priesthood. Here is a wise, reflective, spiritual book affirming celibacy for priests with a charism of celibacy but not demanding it of all."

Dean R. Hoge
Catholic University of America
Washington, D.C.

"Cozzens seeks to free celibacy from its juridical stranglehold. Celibacy is a charism freely given by the Holy Spirit, which is intended to be freely offered to God and the community. Celibacy's charism is total radical self-giving love through life-long abstinence from sexual relations. Ironically, mandating celibacy through Church law makes celibacy an obligation for many who do not have the charism, and offers the false promise that the gift will come through obedience to the law. Can we continue to impose celibacy as a law on diocesan clergy, many of whom do not have the charism? Cozzens mounts historical, theological, and pastoral reasons why the mandate should end."

Kathleen A. Cahalan
Associate Professor
Saint John's University School of Theology
and Seminary

"Cozzens's discussion about *Freeing Celibacy* offers a profound and balanced respect for charismatic celibacy, while laying out a clear case for a return to the early Christian community's equally healthy embrace of a married presbyterate and episcopate. He leads us through questioning John Paul II's mindset that celibacy is 'the pearl of great price which is preferred to every other value no matter how great.' From professional experience, Cozzens provides sharp insights into the dark side of imposed and legislated celibacy and the negative impact it continues to unleash on our church. While highlighting examples of true celibate commitment, Cozzens offers a clear and passionate view of men who know they have been called to priesthood, but are yoked to celibacy as a requisite for continued ministry. His comment that many priests 'sense that God takes no pleasure in their loneliness' rings profoundly with a sense of personal experience. Cozzens's concise history of mandatory celibacy provides a great and readable overview for those who would like to learn more about why it has endured. One is left wondering how we can ever have a priesthood that exhibits authenticity and credibility, or true spiritual leadership, as the norm, while our priests and bishops are kept institutionally celibate."

C. Russell Ditzel
CORPUS
High Bridge, New Jersey

"Donald Cozzens gives the reader much to ponder. In an accessible style with attention both to historical context and theological foundations, he describes the joy and beauty as well as the burden of celibacy. Cozzens recognizes the faithful service of most priests; at the same time, he also recognizes the irony of mandating a gift or charism. He argues convincingly that the restriction against marriage placed upon those who have the charism of priestly ministry but not that of celibacy are unjust. Though the requirement of celibacy and its impact on diocesan priests is the primary focus, lay, ordained, and vowed religious will all find this book to be an insightful reflection on the liberating nature of faithfully living out one's call from God. This deeply honest examination of celibacy should be read by all who strive to lead lives faithful to the baptismal call to bear witness to the Gospel."

Regina Wentzel Wolfe, Ph.D.
Dominican University

DONALD COZZENS

FREEING
CELIBACY

LITURGICAL PRESS
Collegeville, Minnesota

www.litpress.org

1	2	3	4	5	6	7	8

Library of Congress Cataloging-in-Publication Data

Cozzens, Donald B.
    Freeing celibacy / Donald Cozzens.
        p.   cm.
    Includes bibliographical references.
    ISBN-13: 978-0-8146-3160-7 (alk. paper)
    ISBN-10: 0-8146-3160-6 (alk. paper)
    1. Celibacy—Catholic Church.   2. Catholic Church—Clergy.
  I. Title.

BV4390.C69 2006
253'.252—dc22

2006004029

Other Titles by Donald Cozzens

The Changing Face of the Priesthood

Sacred Silence: Denial and the Crisis in the Church

Faith That Dares to Speak

The Spirituality of the Diocesan Priest

IN MEMORY OF

JAMES PATRICK COZZENS

1946–2005

CONTENTS

INTRODUCTION

THIS BOOK HAS BEEN GERMINATING for more than forty years. In fact, it is fair to say I've been wrestling with its substance since I felt called to the priesthood more than sixty years ago as a first grader at Holy Name Elementary School in Cleveland. But even from these early school days my desire to be a priest met with a sense of unease. First-graders are too young for existential angst, but I believe I felt something akin to this pervasive, unsettling anxiety. The source of my unease was another first-grader—and the ensuing twelve year infatuation with JoAnn refused to relax its hold on me until I entered the seminary. To my innocent Catholic imagination, celibacy went with priesthood the way fish went with Friday. I see things a bit differently today.

The present book has been percolating, so to speak, for some five years since Peter Dwyer, the director of Liturgical Press, and I discussed the need for a reflection on the hot-button issue of mandatory celibacy. It reached a boiling point, if you will allow me to mix my metaphors, when I was asked to do an endorsement for a book on celibacy by a noted author for whom I have considerable regard. The author evidenced a profound respect for the priesthood, the church, and for celibacy rightly lived. His manuscript, however, brought me up short. In spite of the author's grasp of the spiritual, psychological, and sacramental character of

1

celibacy and its witness to a sexually obsessed and confused culture, it labored, I thought, under the weight of a serious flaw. The author had intentionally avoided any discussion of what is arguably the core theological issue of celibacy— its requirement by church law for diocesan priests of the Latin rite. Celibacy that rings true, celibacy that is one's truth so to speak, celibacy that fosters a passionate love of God, humanity, and creation, is first and foremost a gift of God's Spirit for the mission of the church. In theological language, it is a charism (a gift), the implications of which we will explore in the chapters that follow, especially chapters two and three.

Wise counsel on how to live a life of celibate chastity with integrity and fidelity must acknowledge the problematic character of mandated or obligatory celibacy. For at the core of celibacy's breakdown—and it is breaking down—is the attempt by the church to mandate a charism. Church officials have for sometime now spoken of celibacy as both a charism and a discipline. If a Catholic (man) feels called to the priesthood, the Holy Spirit, the church proclaims, will bestow the grace necessary for the seminarian and future priest to remain faithful to his promise of celibacy.

Does grace abound? Christians believe it does indeed. But grace builds on nature, and if an individual does not possess the aptitude, temperament, and quality of soul that are the human foundations of charismatic celibacy, calling upon grace to make up for these deficiencies is a manifestation, one can argue, of ecclesial arrogance. A well-respected scholar and seminary professor understood the daunting task of training seminarians for celibate living who do not possess the charism of celibacy. "It is like trying to train people to be ballerinas who can't dance the two-step."

Of course, discerning a charism, whether to celibacy or preaching or counseling or parenthood, is often difficult and the task of a lifetime. Sometimes, like Jeremiah, we come to see the full reality of our gifts and talents (our charisms) only in the autumn of our lives. And of course mystery pervades the working of grace. By God's grace, it is possible, it would seem, to grow into a charism. Or better put, God is free to bestow God's gifts even in the mature years of one's life. Moreover, it is possible to grieve choices not made, opportunities not taken, and at the same time rejoice thankfully in the blessings and joys of the path taken. But, oh, at what price. It seems this is the principle the church is standing on: *Embrace the celibate priesthood whether you feel blessed with the charism of celibacy or not,* it urges its seminarians, *and you will receive the grace to live it faithfully and with joy.*

For numerous priests, that is more or less how things have played out. For others, for many others, celibacy has been an unnecessary, unnatural, and unhealthy burden that has shrunk their souls and drained the last drops of passion from their lives. For still others, while celibacy has proven to be a similar burden, they have found the courage to resist the shrinking of their souls and the extinguishing of their passion. I trust these men will find themselves and their mostly hidden stories of conflict and courage in the pages ahead.

Freeing Celibacy's primary focus is the law of celibacy for diocesan priests. The arc of its concern includes the experience of celibacy of vowed religious: monks and nuns, brothers and sisters. And it acknowledges that some lay people are called to lead celibate lives for the sake of the gospel—Dorothy Day, for example. Still others experience celibacy not as a choice but a reality imposed by life's circumstances. In this book my attention remains on ecclesiastically endorsed and mandated celibacy, the publicly recognized celibacy of diocesan priests.

Let me here acknowledge and give thanks for the companions in faith who have strengthened me and accompanied me on my own celibate journey of preaching, teaching, and writing: My family, who from the very beginning intuitively understood the joys and sorrows, the dignity and peril of celibate priesthood. Their evident joy and pride in their priest son and brother were balanced by their acceptance of me as one not so much set apart but as one of their own. I am grateful for friendships with women religious who never doubted the graced and blessed character of our celibate and transforming love. I give thanks, too, for brother priests who met with me for years and in some cases decades for prayer, faith sharing, and personal truth telling—their honest struggles and brave discipleship made me proud to be a part of their brotherhood.

Over the years I've enjoyed deep friendships with married couples whose warmth and hospitality and human goodness revealed the grace with which they carried the burdens of family life and celebrated the joys and intimacies of their common life. Evenings in their homes and at their tables inevitably renewed my spirit. Students from Ursuline College, Saint Mary Seminary, and John Carroll University gave me hope in the future of our church and society—their search for meaningful lives revealed their spiritual hunger and their love of God. And finally I acknowledge and thank theologians and journalists, too numerous to mention by name, who have dared to tell the truth about the priesthood, about sexuality, about celibacy, about the church's need for renewal and reform. I have been inspired by their example. To all of the above, my heartfelt thanks.

CHAPTER ONE

THE MYSTIQUE OF CELIBACY

Mys·tique, n. an aura of heightened value or interest or meaning surrounding a person or thing.

THERE IS SOMETHING SEXY ABOUT CELIBACY. What could possibly prompt someone to publicly claim that he or she will not marry, not date in the usual sense of the word, and not engage in explicit sexual behaviors? The question itself has a certain allure to it. The curiosity celibacy raises, at least in many people, signals more than mere interest. It signals fascination. What makes these men and women tick? Are they simply misfits—strange, fearful, repressed, reclusive? Many think so. On the other hand, those who get to know integrated, mature celibates sometimes come to the conclusion that celibates might well "make the best lovers." Moreover, healthy, vital celibate people are attractive: not necessarily physically attractive, but with the compelling attractiveness that comes from the contemplative center of the soul—the only place where people come to be at home with themselves.

With notable exceptions, they seem to be less self-absorbed than most and many celibates seem genuinely interested in others. Often they project a spiritual aura that signals it is safe to approach and safe to reveal. Publicly perceived as unavailable for romantic liaisons, the quality of being "off limits," and "out of bounds," at least in some celibates, makes them all the more attractive in the eyes of many. Platonic friendships between celibates and between celibates and non-celibates, freed from the undercurrents of sexual and romantic tensions, are often sources of spiritual insight and simple delight. And where there is sexual attraction, the celibate commitment to non-genital relationships has the capacity to generate transforming, spiritually enriching, and life-defining friendships.

A half century ago Deborah Kerr and Robert Mitchum captured celibacy's sexual allure and mystique in the film *Heaven Knows, Mr. Allison.*[1] Stranded on a Japanese held island during World War II, Kerr as Sister Angela and Mitchum playing the worldly Corporal Allison spend days and nights hiding in one of the island's caves. The chemistry between the two disparate characters thrown into inescapable physical proximity is the underlying motif of the film. Mr. Allison, the only form of address that Sister Angela affords him, finds himself falling for the nun in full habit whose studied propriety and apparent indifference to the romantic and sexual possibilities of their situation only intensifies his attraction. His interest, it seems to me, is more than sexual desire for an attractive young woman. Sister Angela's vowed foreclosure of erotic and romantic fulfillment puzzles Mr. Allison and at the same time captivates him. Without apparent understanding, he has been confronted with the mystique of celibacy, the mystical union of the sensual with the sacred, the flesh with

the transcendent. When these polar elements of life con-
verge, as they do at the most sublime moments of human
desire and self-giving, our finite world touches the infi-
nite. Mr. Allison had never before encountered such a holy
convergence of spirituality, chaste reserve, and physicality.
Rather than his sexual desire degenerating into lust, it is
held in check by respect, even reverence, for the obvious
innocence and goodness, the obvious simplicity and religious faith of Sister Angela.

Celibacy's mystique is romanticized in films like
Going My Way, The Sound of Music, and *The Flying Nun.*
Dramatic films—*On the Waterfront, Shoes of the Fisher-
man, Thornbirds, Mass Appeal*—and the short-lived television series *Nothing Sacred* reflect more subtle and
nuanced portrayals of celibacy's mystique. So do the novels
of Graham Green, Frank O'Connor, J. F. Powers, James
Carroll, and Andrew Greeley.

The mystique of celibacy seems to hold even in secular, consumerist societies instinctively suspicious of denial
and sacrifice. Corporate moguls and hard-nosed busi-
ness people have been heard to say, "I'll do anything for
those nuns." Religious orders of monks and nuns include
among their benefactors individuals who acknowledge
little understanding of the celibate life—but nonetheless
sense something genuine and authentically spiritual there
that deserves support. There is a pull, a difficult to analyze
attraction, to a lifestyle that seems to make no sense to our
modern and post-modern culture. Perhaps celibate people,
at least from time to time, ignite the divine spark commonly believed to lie dormant in the human soul. When
celibacy is their truth, they point to the transcendent, to

the mystery dimension of life itself, to the human hunger for what matters most.

The same dynamic of regard and reverence for individuals foregoing their right to sexual/genital fulfillment can be found throughout history from the Vestal Virgins of Roman antiquity to the monastic movements of the early middle ages to the various modalities of contemporary religious life. Not even the clergy abuse scandals of the last decades of the past century have extinguished respect for the celibate lives of Catholic priests. Celibacy's mystique, the intuitive understanding that there is something special, something mysteriously present in publicly identifiable celibate individuals—especially when celibate life is closely linked to religious faith—is a phenomenon worthy of reflection.

Of course, in the dark shadow cast by the clergy sexual abuse scandals, the mystique of celibacy has waned. Many people no longer place priests on pedestals. Instead of leading lives of holiness, they see them leading lives of self-indulgence. For growing numbers of Catholics, priests are people to be tolerated rather than emulated.

If celibacy in the twenty-first century is ambiguous, it's polar opposite, sexual indulgence, is profoundly so. While arguably the deepest, strongest human desire after life itself, sexuality and sexual behavior nevertheless generate considerable fear and anxiety. Lovers know that loving well entails vulnerability. Even the first signals of sexual interest risk the hurt and humiliation of rejection. We seem to understand without formal instruction that loving involves pain and suffering and that sexual intercourse, by its very nature, makes promises, promises we are not sure we want to make. Add to the inherent possibility of hurt connected with sexual relationships the real pain and wounding associated with many first experiences of sexual contact, particularly abusive, exploitative ones, the attraction/repulsion dynamic is not surprising. Celibacy may be for individuals scarred and wounded by early sexual experiences an invisible cloak of safety from the destructive forces potentially present in sexual encounters. Surveys of vowed religious women reveal that many suffered sexual abuse in one form or another before they entered the convent. Evidence continues to mount that the majority of priests guilty of abusing children and teenagers were themselves sexually abused as minors. In addition to the inherent ambiguity of human sexuality, gay priests wrestle with the church teaching that their orientation is more than ambiguous, that it is intrinsically disordered. For men terrified by the possibility or certitude that they are gay, a celibate priesthood is often appealing. To some extent, it appears, many celibates have found the ambiguity of human sexuality and its concomitant anxiety too much of an existential burden to bear. In this state of soul, the vows and promises made to practice chaste continence are seen as an attractive, even compelling alternative.

Christianity, of course, has long been suspicious of sexuality and quick to praise those who explicitly forego active sexual lives. We find the roots of this suspicion in the spirit/matter dualism that influenced St. Augustine's negative judgment on sexuality—even in the context of married love.[2] The church's calendar of saints is disproportionately heavy with celibate men and women and the few married saints listed usually lived most of their lives as widows and widowers or abstaining from intercourse. To this day in church circles, at least on a theoretical level, spirit trumps nature and the sensual. There is an irony here. Believers acknowledge that sexuality is God's gift, that committed sexual expression in covenanted relationships (i.e., marriage) is holy, and even that married love is sacramental. Yet, large numbers of believers, especially among church authorities, remain deeply suspicious of the sensual and sexual.

At the same time, there is considerable wisdom in cautious, respectful approaches to sexuality. Philosopher and theologian Paul Tillich and others speak of sexual desire as *daimonic*—a reality having the ability either to lift and transport the human spirit or to wound, even destroy it.[3] Other examples of the *daimonic* include wealth, power, fame, ambition, and of interest here, religion. The best of our religious leaders, philosophers, and spiritual writers have warned us to approach these central aspects of life with care and caution. Though fundamentally good or neutral in themselves, these forces have the power to wreak terrible harm. Not only can we make this claim about sexuality, I will assert in the chapters ahead the *daimonic* character of celibacy itself.

Celibacy's mystique goes beyond the human fascination with sex and the intentional foregoing of an active sex life. Especially in the Catholic imagination, the regard and reverence for vowed religious and celibate clergy can be traced to the long history of heroic service and self-sacrificing pastoral care that is typical of Catholic priests, nuns, and brothers. Celibates are perceived as men and women for others. As missionaries, teachers, nurses, and pastors, they have "left all" and risked everything in a heroic response to the gospel. In Camus' terms, they are rebels who refuse to collaborate with the seductive forces of either utopianism or nihilism. Men and women of faith, they struggle to live simply, day by day, acutely aware of their own limitations and the numbing pseudo-values celebrated by their culture. Throughout the centuries many have suffered to the point of martyrdom in the pastoral care of their people and in fidelity to the human struggle for justice and peace. Many more have gained the status of elders: men and women whose life-long fidelity to the word of God and unquestioned authenticity has led others to see them as wisdom figures. These are the bigger-than-life members of religious orders and congregations. These are the pastors grandparents tell their grandchildren about. These are the teachers remembered at class reunions. To greater and lesser degrees, and with many sad and even tragic exceptions, their witness to the gospel enlightened and encouraged and, not infrequently, transformed countless lives.

The newly ordained and recently professed religious know that the respect they receive, from Catholics and often from non-Catholics, has yet to be earned. It comes their way because of those who have gone before them. Moreover, they understand they are part of a tradition that has shaped and sustained this mystique—that they stand on the shoulders of those who have gone before them. Mystique, they begin to understand, emerges slowly, refined in the crucible of unselfish service and heroic struggle of a group or profession. It has been created, if you will, by others long dead and often forgotten.

Another factor contributing to celibacy's mystique is the intentional gender blurring characteristic of male clergy and religious. Men in dress-like cassocks, flowing robes, lace vestments, and embroidered capes have for centuries fostered an androgynous clerical milieu. When explicit sexual gender is suppressed in the service of sustaining celibate continence a mystique does indeed emerge. But it is ultimately unsuccessful, unhealthy, and susceptible to perversion. In some clerics, behaviors emerge that are classic examples of camp and dandyism,[4] and, as we shall see in chapter seven, this is an environment especially attractive to some gay men and others confused about their sexual identity.

With the exception of the environs of Rome close to the Vatican, the sight of black-robed priests has declined dramatically since the Second Vatican Council. Still, the image of priests in cassocks remains steadfast in the Catholic imagination of middle-aged and older believers. The androgynous dress, in turn, was complemented by the androgynous demeanor and style of numerous clergy. Just who were these men? What made them tick? Were they God's chosen or simply strange? In anti-clerical circles, the response to such questions was emphatically derisive. Yet among the faithful, a certain reverence for the mystery and sacred dignity of the priesthood was passed from generation to generation. Added to this reverence and fascination was the overlay of aristocratic privilege, power, and secrecy associated with clerical culture. Working class sons were suddenly members of the church's aristocracy—with comforts and status that seemed to more than make up for the imposed celibacy of the priesthood. The institution of celibacy—with its androgynous, asexual tenor—

eventually became grounded on a rock-solid foundation buttressed by theological, spiritual, political, economic, cultural, and institutional ramparts. It was a fortress of considerable strength.

The androgynous character of the priesthood notwithstanding, and in spite of the celibacy requirement, vocations to the priesthood were abundant in the middle decades of the twentieth century. And many of these recruits for the priesthood were unambiguously masculine. Not a few were veterans of World War II, men with generous hearts seasoned and sobered by the rigors and horrors of armed conflict. They believed they knew what really mattered and eagerly embraced the mysterious call to priesthood and ministry. Others came from the farms, while the majority arrived at seminary gates from cities not yet thinned by suburban sprawl. Since grace, Christians believe, builds on nature, this generation of seminarians as well as others were attracted, at least in part, to the mystery, grandeur, and power intimately linked to ordination—to what I have referred to here as the mystique of the celibate priesthood.

In addition to the promise of celibacy (a condition for ordination), diocesan priests promise their bishop obedience and at the same time commit themselves to lives of gospel simplicity. Religious order priests, of course, take vows of poverty, chastity (understood as celibate continence), and obedience. While the mystique of the priesthood is grounded in the mystique of celibacy, it is reinforced by the equally counter-cultural commitments to obedience and simplicity of life (the vow of poverty of religious priests). In societies shaped by the Enlightenment values of rational self-determination, independence, and liberty, obedience to a bishop, abbot, or religious superior can be as puzzling as the forgoing of sexual and human fulfillment in marriage. This is especially the case when the obedience has a quasi-military character. Such surrender of individual will raises the same questions associated with celibacy. What kind of men and women are these? Is their commitment to the church's mission heroic or masochistic? Do they possess an otherworldly wisdom or are they simply naïve? Are they to be admired or pitied? In the eyes of many, the obedience of priests and religious is as fascinating and perplexing as celibacy.

Theologian and spiritual writer Ronald Rolheiser has proposed that those who sleep alone are poor.[5] Celibacy, from this perspective, is a kind of poverty. The celibate trusts that the human intimacy that he or she needs as a finite, limited creature will be provided, will come in ways not manipulated or controlled. As the poor often wait for daily bread, celibates wait, without willful maneuvering, for the human connectedness essential for the life of their souls. Physical poverty is nothing to be romanticized. It carries no aura of mystique. Emotional poverty, on the other hand, trusting that one's human need for relationship and communion will ultimately be met, is a different matter. The vowed poverty of celibate religious and the simplicity of life common to committed celibate priests are a constant challenge and countersign to any culture of consumption. When celibacy is understood as emotional poverty, a state in life making no public declaration, no claim that another is one's spouse or covenanted partner, its fundamental mystique is deepened.

Society's fascination with the Catholic priesthood, a fascination that extends far beyond the Catholic community, is closely linked, I have proposed here, with the mystique of celibacy. If celibacy were not required of priests, it is reasonable to ask, would the public's enduring interest in the priesthood be diminished? Is the mystique of celibacy so intimately connected with the mystique of the priesthood itself that the mystery and allure of the ordained, undoubtedly weakened in recent decades, would be further eroded to the point of extinction? Many today fear it would. Moreover, they believe that without mandatory celibacy priests would become even more middle class than they already are—at least in the minds of some. These individuals insist that without obligatory celibacy priests would lose what little "fire in the belly" they currently possess, that they would be even less prophetic and countercultural to a society awash in secular values.

While there are other arguments for maintaining mandatory celibacy for diocesan priests of the Latin rite, as we will see in the chapters ahead, celibacy's mystique should not be judged inconsequential.

Faithful response to the charism of celibacy, we will see in the following chapter, is one of the church's great treasures. Like other charisms, it is to be honored and respected. At the same time, when celibacy is imposed and legislated it can undermine the integrity of the church's leadership and cause needless human suffering. If charismatic celibacy is indeed a jewel in the crown of the priesthood, mandated, obligatory celibacy for individuals not blessed with the charism is a silent martyrdom.

CHAPTER TWO

CELIBACY AS CHARISM

Char·ism, n. a gift freely given by God to a person or community, for the good and service of others in bringing about the Reign of God.

"When I run," said British Olympic sprinter Eric Liddell, "I feel God's pleasure." Liddell, played by Ian Charleson in the Oscar winning film *Chariots of Fire*, acknowledged with these simple words that his world-class athletic skill was fundamentally God's gift.[1] While it isn't clear that he thought of his exceptional speed as directly contributing to the building up of the reign of God, Liddell rightly understood that his intention to use his giftedness for the glory of God made his running somehow sacred. And he felt the presence of God, felt God's very pleasure. There is an implicit act of humility in this insight. This is no vain boast on Liddell's part, but a declaration that he has been gifted, and using his gift with the right intentionality, in itself, pleased God. Not to run, not to compete, was unthinkable. Unused gifts, the missionary Liddell knew from his theological studies, frustrate the divine plan and, to a greater or lesser degree, shrink the human soul.

Since believers commonly hold that grace builds on nature, they understand a charism as building on a natural aptitude for a specific behavior or way of life. In theory, at least, monks possess an aptitude for monastic life, married people for family life and parenthood, teachers for developing the art of questioning, scientists for research. It is only a small stretch to concede that calls to monasticism, parenthood, teaching, research, writing, and other vocations are rightly understood, from a theological perspective, as charisms—as gifts from the divinity for the welfare of society, for personal fulfillment of the one gifted, and for the glory of God. Temperament, personality, intellectual bent, kinetic ability, genetic predisposition all coalesce in the emerging charism. Charisms, therefore, are graced abilities grounded in natural gifts and human potential ordained for the common good, for the building of the Kingdom of God. Moreover, they shape the destiny of the recipient. His or her spiritual and personal development remains intimately linked to how one respects, develops, and responds to the gifts bestowed.

Like Eric Liddell, at least from time to time, the exercise of God-given gifts and talents humbles the human actor who finds aptitudes and abilities embedded in his or her body/spirit. Preachers blessed with the charism of preaching experience the same mysterious, uncanny awareness of "God's pleasure" when they preach. Not always, of course, but sometimes. The same can be said of teachers, artists, administrators, counselors, and pastors, to name some of the more obvious gifts of the Spirit given for the common good and the building up of the reign of God. The same, we might add, can be said of any human activity—work, play, service, prayer—done with awareness, mindfulness, and reverent attention. For the believer, life itself is the fundamental charism to be "used" for the glory of God and the welfare of society. At different times, individuals of all ages, temperaments, and dispositions may sense that their very living gives God pleasure.

Possessing a charism, a gifted predisposition for outstanding achievement or performance, does not mean that the exercise of the gift is effortless. Liddell trained strenuously to bring himself to the point of optimal conditioning for his 1924 Olympic races. Charismatic preachers study Scripture and theology, literature and the arts in general, in order to proclaim God's liberating and transforming word to contemporary ears. Gifted teachers prepare long and hard to capture the attention and imagination of their students. Musicians and actors rehearse untold hours to hone and develop their talents and skills. Charisms are anything but a free pass from the discipline and toil of preparation and practice. They remain, however, the foundations of graced ministry, performance, and achievement.

Some few men and women appear to possess the charism of celibacy, a graced call from God to pledge themselves to celibate living for the good of others and for the building up in history of the reign of God. For these individuals, celibacy is their *truth*—the right way for them to live out their lives. Without disparaging marriage and with regard for the goodness and wholesomeness of human sexuality, they sense a mysterious pull of grace toward singleness that seems to fit with their inner life and spiritual journey. It is mysterious because it often makes no sense even to themselves, let alone to their family and friends. It is a pull—like being drawn by a magnet—because it is not necessarily, at least in the beginning of their discernment, their choice. As the Dutch theologian Edward Schillebeeckx once said of the celibate: he or she has an "existential inability to do otherwise." Celibates sense, moreover, that herein lies the key to their spiritual freedom, and that fidelity to this mysterious, perplexing gift is all important. Intuitively, they sense that their gift of celibacy is linked to the mission of building up the Kingdom of God. Charisms, by their nature, are not given for the fulfillment of the individual alone but for the welfare and betterment of others—for the sake of the gospel.

Consider that roughly half of the world's population is unmarried. Widows and widowers, the divorced and separated, adults whose circumstances have precluded marriage, find themselves living outside of marriage. Some, disillusioned with marriage or tired of the stress and tensions of dating, proclaim themselves, more or less seriously, "celibates."[2] Celibacy, as discussed here, is, of course, much more than not being married. It is the decision, I have emphasized, to live out one's life without spouse for the greater good of the gospel. For the person who has received this charism, it is the best way, if not the only way, to live out his or her life. As commonly understood, the charism of celibacy implies sexual continence, the forgoing of all deliberate sexual experience. In most cases, there is a public, social dimension to recognized celibacy such as public vows or ordination to the priesthood in the Latin rite. While it is true that true holiness is evident in the ordinary lives of countless single men and women, they are seldom acknowledged as celibates by the larger community of believers. Charisms, however, refuse to be strictly delineated. Dorothy Day, by way of example, the heroic social activist, pacifist, and co-founder of the Catholic Worker, lived a devout, celibate life, bearing extraordinary witness to gospel values following her conversion to Catholicism. Many would hold that Day's celibacy was charismatic.

Gifts, understood in the religious sense of charism, are seldom realized or claimed beyond all doubt. When they *are* claimed by individuals, the assertion itself creates doubt. It seems more in harmony with the working of grace that one believes he or she has received the charism. More often than not, the charism is confirmed by the faith community as a gift to the church for the mission of the church. In the case of celibacy, I have heard priests say that they have *come to believe* that their "truth" is celibacy. But this understanding often comes after many years of pastoring and well into the autumn of their lives. These men understand that the gift of celibacy does not mean that sexual abstinence is easy, without struggle or temptations, without loneliness. Nor does the charism of celibacy mean that they never long for the companionship of marriage, for children, for the warmth of family life. Charismatic celibates have come to believe that the mystery of grace has called them to lead lives of celibate chastity for the sake of the reign of God. This belief goes hand in hand with doubt. But the belief holds.

Because we are discussing here the mystery of grace, charismatic celibacy as described above is a little too facile. The "charism of celibacy" remains a construct. It is a human attempt to understand an apparent divine design that prompts and allows red-blooded men and women to lead

healthy, full lives without the support and consolation of
a husband or wife. It anticipates our discussion in chapter
three that examines the implications of institutional celibacy, that is, mandatory or obligatory celibacy for diocesan
priests of the Latin rite. For the present discussion, a number of questions arise.

Are charisms in general, and the charism of celibacy
in particular, necessarily permanent gifts? Can an individual be called to celibate living for a specific period of time?
Can the gift of celibacy die a natural death? Can a priest
grow into authentic celibate living who first embraced it
for less than healthy reasons—for example, fear of mature, sexual intimacy or fear of the commitment entailed in
marriage? Many if not most priests, I have come to think,
are reluctant to claim the charism of celibacy—even when
they have led authentic celibate lives that have deepened
their humanity and enhanced their preaching and pastoral ministry. A fundamental ambiguity remains. Many say
they would marry if given the freedom to do so. Others,
often depending on their age, think not. Still others would
not even consider the option to marry. A large number
of priests, I suspect, would say they're not sure, that they
need to pray about it, to test the idea with friends and
spiritual guides. While many priests may hesitate to either claim or disclaim the charism of celibacy, most would
claim the charism of priesthood. Priesthood, they believe,
is their truth, their calling. What is less clear is the right-
ness, the fit of their celibate state.

Bishop John Crowley of the diocese of Middlesbrough in the
U.K., addressed the deep tension priests experience when

they feel called to both priesthood and marriage. On the oc-
casion of his fortieth anniversary of ordination, he expressed
the personal hope that within his lifetime "the church might
more generally allow married priests." Crowley is right to
say "more generally," because there are hundreds of married Latin rite priests who, upon converting to Catholicism
from ministerial roles in Anglican and Protestant denominations, have been dispensed from the law of celibacy. Writing in *The Tablet,* Crowley offered the following reflection
on his life as a celibate.

> I would want to sing my song in favor of celibacy as *one*
> blessed route to living priesthood. How could I do otherwise
> when, having just clocked up forty years as a celibate priest,
> I personally have found it such a grace from God? Like any
> other celibate, I could tell of the times when that call from
> God has seemed to cost not less than everything. No need
> to expatiate on the seasons of struggle, the sometimes pro-
> found aching within, when the human heart feels all the
> God-given drive towards the most intimate union with one
> other. That is how we are gloriously made, and there is no
> need to labor that side of the celibacy *challenge.*
>
> Rather, let me labor a little the other side of the celibacy
> *opportunity.* For me, and for countless others, it has of-
> fered deep down a possibility of that kind of relationship
> with the person of Jesus as friend and brother, which is
> life-giving, joyous and—potentially—transforming. Read
> that last sentence by the way within the real context that
> (and this I imagine is also true within a good marriage)
> you simply get on with the day-to-day routine of being
> faithful in word and deed to the other.[3]

As Crowley proposes, there are countless priests who have learned how to make celibacy "work." Through struggle, prayer, and commitment, and through grace-filled, life-giving friendships with both men and women, they have deepened their humanity and their effectiveness as bearers of the Word.

While there is indeed a mystique to celibacy, there are characteristics commonly found in the lives of healthy celibates well into their senior years. While these qualities are present to healthy, altruistic individuals of every age and walk of life they are the markers of authentic charismatic celibacy. Let me to tell you of an elderly woman who embodied many of these characteristics. While teaching at Ursuline College in Cleveland during the 1980s, I had the good fortune to meet an Ursuline nun by the name of Kilian Hufgard. She graciously agreed to tutor me in the history and theory of art and architecture from the perspective of St. Bernard of Clairvaux, the great inspiration of her life. Almost a generation older than I, Sister Kilian spoke quietly—but with undeniable passion—about things well made, about the transcendent quality of that which is good, about the dynamics and mystery of human creativity. She was, I believe, the most fascinating woman I have ever met. There was no doubt in my mind that she possessed not only the heart and soul of an artist and scholar but also the gift of celibacy. I believe what defined her life as a vowed religious and celibate is characteristic of charismatic celibates in general.

Sr. Kilian demonstrated a freedom of soul, an at-homeness, an at-easeness, that put others at ease in her company. She was a woman at peace with herself. Like healthy, integrated celibates, she welcomed others without judgment and those who came into the circle of her presence were touched by the ease and peace she radiated. Keenly aware of the fundamental goodness of creation and things well made, Sr. Kilian radiated a consistent spirit of reverence. She was alert to the divine spark present in all manifestations of reality, especially in the most humble of creatures. Most charismatic celibates display a similar reverence in their human interactions and in their approach to nature and the created world.

Charismatic celibates exhibit a spirit of gratitude. Like Dorothy Day and Sr. Kilian, they sense the hidden drama of grace unfolding in both the ordinary moments of life as well as the more critical, life-shaping events that mark our lives. With French novelist Georges Bernanos' country priest, they understand that "all is grace." Building upon this insight, they see blessing upon blessing. Because celibacy itself is perceived as a blessing, they are seldom tempted to self-pity. When their solitude gives way to unmitigated loneliness, when they long for the companionship of their dearest, distant friends, when their celibacy makes no sense whatever, they trust that their darkness of soul will pass. With believers everywhere, with married, single, and separated, they see that indeed "all is grace."

Sr. Kilian greeted her visitors with unconditional hospitality. In her presence, one felt truly welcomed—sincerely, warmly welcomed. A visit with her, no matter how brief, left me with the feeling that I had just been blessed. In her final years, Dorothy Day left her visitors with the same sense of blessing. Paul Elie, in his acclaimed *The Life*

You Save May Be Your Own, captured this arresting presence: "Now she was a holy person, who inspired others to come to see her, to be in her presence, to enjoy the favor it bestowed, and to recall the encounter precisely."[4] Without the leveling potential inherent in marriage, celibates may easily become self-absorbed and more or less taken with their special status. Whenever this is the case, their ability to extend hospitality is diminished. Healthy, charismatic celibates, like Hufgard and Day, resist this tendency. Their own centeredness, the result of their unwavering integrity and radical commitment, make them masters of graced hospitality.

Finally, if we look closely, many of the celibates we may know turn out to be some of the most passionate people we know. They are far from the asexual, otherworldly, slightly weird individuals portrayed in film and television sit-coms. Their passion, uncluttered by the simplicity of their lives and filtered through the strain of contemplative awareness, unmasks a thirst for life in its fullness. They have come to know the truest, deepest, longings of their hearts. And so freed from the created, false thirsts of superficial culture, their great frustration is with all that is unreal. When I have been in their presence, I imagine a bumper sticker that reads: "Celibates make the best lovers."

Certainly these characteristics are found wherever individuals, regardless of their celibate or married status, endeavor to live lives of integrity and genuine concern for others. They remain, I believe, signs that a publicly committed celibate man or woman may indeed be the recipient of what the church deems the charism of celibacy.

We have had a glimpse into the lives of two healthy, life-giving celibates, Ursuline Sister Kilian Hufgard and the social activist and writer Dorothy Day. Each woman, beyond their noteworthy and exceptional accomplishments, is perceived as thoroughly real. Though no longer among the living, they ring true. Most believers, I suspect, know of celibate men and women who have touched their lives in meaningful ways, sometimes in profound ways. Wherever and whenever we encounter such individuals, the value and blessing of celibacy is vindicated and strengthened. True celibates remind us of what really matters, of what matters most in life. They remind us of the mysterious ways of grace—that different paths may be equally valid choices in living out one's fidelity to the gospel; that what appears to be unhealthy self-abnegation in the eyes of many might indeed be one's liberating truth. Healthy, charismatic celibates will be some of the most spiritually liberated people we will ever meet. For these believers, celibacy is indeed freeing.

CHAPTER THREE

CELIBACY AS OBLIGATION

Tau·tol·o·gy, n. a statement which is true by its own definition, and is therefore fundamentally uninformative, e.g., lying is wrong because it is a sin.

Canon 277—Clerics are obliged to observe perfect and perpetual continence for the sake of the kingdom of heaven and therefore are obliged to observe celibacy, which is a special gift of God, by which sacred ministers can adhere more easily to Christ with an undivided heart and can more freely dedicate themselves to the service of God and humankind.

IT WOULD BE MORE ACCURATE AND HONEST if Canon 277 read, "*Since the twelfth century* clerics have been obliged to observe perfect and perpetual continence . . . and therefore are obliged to observe celibacy. . . ." Not until the Lateran Councils (1123 and 1139) did clerical celibacy become the norm for the entire Western or Latin church. Yet so deeply is clerical celibacy ingrained in the Catholic collective consciousness that it is only in the second half of the twentieth century that the law in the post-medieval era has received widespread, critical attention and calls for repeal. Defenders of mandated, institutional celibacy point to much earlier laws requiring celibacy for priests, for

31

example in fourth and fifth century Spain, but these regulations were for local churches, not the universal church.[1] During this same period, married priests and bishops were often encouraged to abstain from marital relations with their wives, especially the night before celebrating mass. In spite of local prohibitions to clerical marriage, restrictions on the conjugal rights of married priests and bishops, and considerable popular support for clerical celibacy, the right of priests to marry, indeed the right of bishops and popes to marry, was acknowledged and honored.

For more than half of its two-thousand-year history, in the face of passionate assertions by saintly scholars and popes of the superiority of virginity over sexual expression even in marriage, priests were free to marry. And they still are in Eastern Europe where the Latin law prohibiting clerical marriage does not hold force. From the earliest centuries of Christianity when Eastern churches were intellectually and culturally preeminent, a married clergy was the norm. And to this day, Eastern Catholic churches (e.g., Byzantine, Coptic, Maronite rite churches in full communion with Rome) permit their priests to marry as long as they do so before ordination.[2] Moreover, as we shall see in the next chapter, there are hundreds (exact numbers have not been made public by the church) of married Latin rite priests actively engaged in ministry.[3] Ordained clergy, mostly from the Anglican/Episcopal Church, they converted to Catholicism and, after relatively short periods of seminary instruction, were ordained as Catholic priests. In most cases, it appears their wives and children converted at the time of their husbands' and fathers' entrance into the Catholic communion.[4]

Clearly, the tradition of married priests, bishops, and popes of the first millennium and the current practice of receiving Anglican and other married ministers into full communion with the Catholic Church dispels the claim of some traditionalist Catholics that celibacy is essential to the priesthood. Strictly speaking, the issue for growing numbers of Catholics today is not optional celibacy for priests, but, as Bishop Crowley suggested, a more general expansion of a practice that is already a respected reality in Eastern churches and in limited fashion in the Latin rite itself. Indeed, if we concede that healthy, life-giving celibacy is a charism given by God to relatively few individuals, mandatory celibacy emerges as an oxymoron. Gifts that are grounded in the grace of God simply cannot be legislated.

Yet the church continues to insist that the gift of "chastity in absolute and perpetual celibacy" can be the subject of law. In the apostolic exhortation of Pope John Paul, *I Will Give You Shepherds*, the case for the law of celibacy is drawn from an earlier papal exhortation. *"In virginity and celibacy, the human being is awaiting . . . the eschatological marriage of Christ with the Church, giving himself or herself completely to the Church in the hope that Christ may give himself to the Church in the full truth of eternal life."*[5] Building on this less than clear assertion, the pope continues. *"In this light one can appreciate the reasons behind the centuries-old choice which the Western Church has made and maintained—despite all the difficulties and objections raised down the centuries—of conferring the Order of Presbyter only on men who have given proof that they have been called by God to the gift of chastity in absolute and perpetual celibacy."*[6]

only celibate can be ordained not ord, then celibate

Only two paragraphs later, John Paul speaks of the law of celibacy affirming the church's right to legislate the charism of celibate chastity. "It is especially important that the priest understand the theological motivation of the Church's law on celibacy. Inasmuch as it is a law, it expresses *the Church's will,* even before the will of the subject expressed by his readiness. But the will of the Church finds its ultimate motivation in the *link between celibacy and sacred Ordination,* which configures the priest to Jesus Christ the Head and the Spouse of the Church."[7] The conflation here of charism and law is asserted without the least indication that the argument for the both/and nature of celibacy (both charism and law) is theologically problematic and logically contorted. For many who struggle to understand the theology and logic expressed here, it comes down to this—it is so because the church says it is so.

Imagine for a moment a church that required celibacy of its ordained ministers from the second century on. We would see a church with a strikingly different roster of saints and popes. St. Augustine, the architect of Christianity's negative view of human sexuality, found a platform for his scholarship and teaching as the secretary and spokesperson for Pope Damasus I, the son of a bishop. Two centuries earlier, the son of a priest became Pope Sixtus (c. 116–125). Moreover, saints who were popes begot sons who became popes and saints. Pope St. Anastasius I (399–401) was succeeded by his son, Pope St. Innocent I (401–417). A century later, Pope St. Hormisdas (514–523) fathered a son who became Pope St. Silverius (536–537). The feast days of these married saints linked by the highest church office and family ties remain off the General Roman Calendar. Is the reason behind this omission fear that the public recognition of their saintly, married lives might further the cause of optional celibacy? The great pope and doctor of the church of the late sixth century, Gregory I, was the great-grandson of Pope Felix III and a great-great-grandson of Pope Felix II. Gregory, it should be noted, proposed that celibacy, replacing martyrdom, was the great witness to Christ and the gospel. Approximately a dozen popes in the first millennium were sons of priests. Let me conclude this brief retrospective with mention of Pope Adrian II (867–872), the last married pope.[8] He was not an anomaly as we have seen, but one of a line of husbands and fathers, many of whom were acclaimed as saints, to have served the church as bishops of Rome.

The number of married bishops and priests in the first twelve centuries is beyond reckoning. So is the number of celibate bishops and priests in the first millennium. But for those married, may we not assume that they felt called both to ordained ministry and to marriage? Are we to conclude that around the time of the Lateran Councils, God decided to no longer call to the priesthood those who were called to marriage—with the exception of priestly candidates for the Eastern churches? Can we argue, as some still do today, that a call to marriage is incompatible with the call to ordained ministry—as if one cancels out the other?

Aware of the conundrum surrounding the legislating of a charism, some church authorities take the position that it is best to address clerical celibacy as a discipline that the church deems well suited to priestly ministry. The law of celibacy, they propose, is an ancient, ascetical tradition that is most fitting in an age so conflicted by its obsession with sex and the near absence of sexual norms. Celibacy for priests, they contend, bears witness to gospel values and to the very witness of Jesus. Moreover, it frees the priest from the cares and demands of marriage and children allowing a more wholehearted, undivided commitment to the pastoral care of the faithful. At the same time, the discipline of obligatory, institutional celibacy for priests safeguards the church from the tragedies that inevitably touch some marriages: infidelity, estrangement, divorce, spousal abuse, child abuse.

It's just better this way, the argument goes, and besides, the church can't afford a married clergy. Priests' salaries would have to be raised and when housing costs and health and retirement benefits are factored in, the financial burdens on parishes would be considerable. The counterpoint to this last concern is the position that the church cannot afford *not* to relax the law of celibacy. While there is no incontrovertible evidence that celibacy is a causal factor in clergy sexual abuse of minors, the psycho-sexual immaturity evident in celibate priests in general and priest-abusers in particular must be considered.[9] The scandal's billion dollar plus cost to the church, it can be argued, takes the steam out of the economic argument against optional celibacy.

From the beginning, financial and property concerns played a significant role in the development of institutional or mandatory celibacy. When married priests died, their wives and children in many cases were reluctant to leave their home, the parish house or rectory. Land held by the church was in some cases claimed by the priest's family with embarrassing legal battles ensuing. When the church's feudal structure is taken into account, the entanglements prove formidable. In place from the tenth century on, dioceses and parishes were awarded to bishops and pastors as a medieval benefice, a fiefdom. The recipient of such a benefice enjoyed the exercise of *dominium*, discretionary control and use of the resources attached to his diocese or parish without the least accountability and transparency to the Catholic community.[10] The current financial scandals rocking the church in the first years of the twenty-first century are traceable to the church's feudal structure where accountability is upwards, only upwards, and without specificity. In feudal systems, lines of accountability and financial disclosure were unheard of. Barring only public heresy or the most outrageous public immorality, a bishop or pastor was granted broad latitude in the administration of his diocese or parish as long as his ecclesiastical assessments and taxes were paid in due course. Little wonder that many contemporary bishops and pastors resent lay oversight of church finances and the accountability and transparency called for by the National Review Board and today's informed laity.[11]

Beneath the weighty issues of property and money reinforcing mandated celibacy lay long-held pagan and early Christian convictions about sex shaped by Manichaean, gnostic, and other dualistic philosophies popular in the early centuries of the first millennium. Both spiritual and philosophical excellence, according to these systems of thought, were to be found in the practice of asceticism and especially in sexual abstinence.[12] The influence of these dualistic philosophies can be traced down through the ages to John Paul II. Commenting on Jesus' teaching in Matthew 19:12 ("There are eunuchs who have been so from birth, and there are eunuchs who have been castrated by others, and there are eunuchs who have castrated themselves for the sake of the kingdom of heaven. Let anyone accept this teaching who can."), John Paul writes, "That preference given to celibacy and virginity 'for the kingdom' was an absolute novelty in comparison with the Old Covenant tradition. . . . Does Christ perhaps suggest the superiority of continence for the kingdom of heaven to matrimony? Certainly."[13]

Sex, like most good things in life, is dangerous. It can extol and expand the human spirit, assuage the deepest of human longings, tease us with a taste of divine ecstasy. At the same time, philosophers of every age confirm our common-sense awareness that sex can restrict the human spirit, compound our human loneliness, and lead to the violent abuse of bodies and souls. We would be wise, we know in our hearts, to be wary of sex. At the same time, we know we would be wise to be grateful for and respectful of this mysterious gift of God. It is fair to criticize the church when it comes to sex. It is also fair to acknowledge the church as the bearer of considerable wisdom in matters of human sexuality. In spite of its obsessive preoccupation with sex and its almost paranoid fear of sex—a fear and suspicion that has scarred untold thousands of believers—the church's heritage of wise and prudent counsel in matters sexual deserves our attention and reflection. Although it took the church more than a millennium to recognize marriage as a sacrament—a means for husband and wife to encounter the living Christ in their shared life, especially in their moments of deepest intimacy—it now attests not only to the fundamental goodness of sex, but to sex's potential to be holy. At the same time, the church teaches that all deliberate sexual thoughts, desires, and actions outside of marriage are seriously sinful and contrary to the divine plan.

   We see here the church's ambiguity toward sex—it is either sin or sacrament. Its insistence on mandatory celibacy for priests suggests that the church has failed to heed and trust its own inspired teaching on the fundamental goodness of human sexuality. The church embodies what it calls *incarnational theology*, the belief that the Word has become flesh, that the divine can be touched in the ordinariness of everyday life, that nature is revelatory of the divine plan, of the Godhead itself. Sadly, perhaps tragically, the church has one ear cocked to hear the word of God, the other attuned to the pagan, dualistic anthropologies (spirit versus matter) that have influence even to this day. The church continues to insist on its own cult of vestal virgins.[14]

From an administrative point of view, there is little doubt that mandated celibacy for priests has proven to be efficient. Church authorities are able to move or transfer priests with almost military precision and efficiency. At ordination, the newly ordained priest kneels before his bishop, places his folded hands in the hands of the ordaining prelate, and promises respect and obedience to him and his successors. In a rite adopted from the feudal ritual of allegiance, the priest in effect acknowledges the bishop as his liege lord. This pledge of loyalty and obedience on the part of the priest/vassal to his lord/bishop establishes and confirms what has proven to be on one of the world's best systems of authority, of command and control. There is no wife for the priest to consult when faced with a new church assignment, no concern for the schooling of children, no home to put on the market. There is little if any negotiation. Theoretically, the move can be effected as soon as the priest can gather his belongings and conclude his pastoral affairs. While consultation with priests before new assignments has expanded greatly since the Second Vatican Council, and priests may decline a move for weighty reasons, celibacy makes clergy personnel appointments a relatively smooth operation. Administratively, celibacy is a great boon to a bishop. Efficiency here trumps effectiveness—to the detriment of the church and great numbers of its priests.

From the perspective of the celibate priest, the church controls the totality of his life. Michael Crosby's 1996 book *Celibacy* is subtitled *Means of Control or Mandate of the Heart?*, which captures the tension implicit in understanding celibacy as fundamentally a charism, a mandate of the heart, or as a mandate of church law. The newly ordained priest soon discovers that the church/bishop controls what he wears, where he lives, what he does, and most especially, his sexuality. For some this is release from adult responsibility for which they are, unfortunately, grateful. Most, I suspect, see this wide-ranging control a shrinking of their spirit and humanity.

The majority of priests love doing what priests do— preaching, celebrating eucharist and the other sacraments, meeting the pastoral needs of parishioners. But consciously or unconsciously, they resent the radical control church authority exercises over their lives—a control that hinders their growth into full, mature adulthood. Let me acknowledge that a large minority of priests would disagree strongly with the picture just drawn of ecclesiastical control. Many of those in disagreement may enjoy the charism of celibacy and find the clerical structure of authority conducive to the humility and simplicity of life called for by the gospel. For these men celibacy is their truth and in obedience to their bishop they find spiritual freedom. Others, I suspect the majority, see it otherwise. For these priests, the experience of obligatory celibacy is far from a necessary cross. They suspect that their spiritual freedom has been restricted rather than expanded by the obligation, that the deference of the laity tends to inflate their egos, that their more or less innocent compensations move them away from gospel simplicity. Deep in their center, they sense that God takes no pleasure in their loneliness. Late at night, in the quiet of their room where it is safe to put aside the priestly persona, they wonder what their spiritual experience would be if the obligation were lifted, an obligation that seems "to cost not less than everything."[15]

CHAPTER FOUR

CELIBACY'S EXCEPTIONS

IN THE SPRING OF 2001, while I was still adjusting to the ups and downs of sharp disapproval and significant acclaim that followed the publication of my book, *The Changing Face of the Priesthood,* I had a moment alone with a Vatican archbishop who had just delivered a lecture at the university where I am teaching. At a dinner party following his presentation, the prelate put his hands under my elbows and guided me into a corner for a private word. He spoke softly, almost in a whisper. "I've read your book," he said, adding, "and I liked it." I nodded my gratitude. "And they are reading it in the Vatican. They think you want optional celibacy." Yes, I thought, that is how it would be read. "I would like to see optional celibacy discussed," I responded—matching the archbishop's *sotto voce.*

It was, on reflection, an exquisite moment that captured the essence of clerical culture. Our simple exchange had had an air of secrecy about it. Though hardly conspiratorial, it was best that our conversation not be overheard. We had been discussing an issue the Vatican did not want discussed.

The criticism *The Changing Face of the Priesthood* had provoked was focused on but two of the nine chapters in the book: the chapter treating the growing numbers of gay men in the priesthood and in our seminaries and the chapter on the mounting scandal of clergy sexual abuse of minors and children. My own presbyteral council (the two dozen or so priests both elected and appointed to offer counsel to the bishop) called me to one of their meetings, heard my "defense," and then rendered their verdict: *The Changing Face of the Priesthood*, they acknowledged, had raised valid, real issues, but they should not have been raised by a "sitting rector."[1] (At the time the book was published, I was president-rector of Saint Mary Seminary and Graduate School of Theology in the Cleveland diocese.) In the United States, controversy had been swirling around the neuralgic issues of sexual orientation and clergy sexual abuse for some time. The Vatican was concerned because both issues were linked in the minds of many with celibacy, and, it was feared, the controversy might weaken the church's position on mandated celibacy for diocesan priests. Church authorities perceived the workings of a liberal agenda behind the issues addressed in my book on the priesthood—even though calls for review of mandated celibacy go beyond the so-called progressive and liberal members of the clergy and laity. *The Changing Face of the Priesthood* did indeed raise thorny, troubling issues—issues, in my judgment, that should no longer, could no longer, be denied.[2]

Obligatory celibacy, we have seen, has been a controversial, conflicted issue throughout the church's long history. In modern times it surfaced with considerable force following the Second Vatican Council, picking up momentum as the Boston abuse scandal erupted in January of 2002. Polls revealed that the majority of the laity and a clear majority of priests were in favor of optional celibacy.

Furthermore, some thirty American bishops publicly expressed their approval of the ordination of married men. The urgent need to examine celibacy's place as a cornerstone of the priesthood appeared to most Catholics and a growing number of bishops to be irrefutable.

Sociologist Richard Schoenherr's research indicated that "Growing minorities of bishops and the majority of theologians, priests, and laypersons agree that both celibacy and marriage should be permitted in the priesthood."[3] Still, the issue of optional celibacy in the Latin rite, in spite of the drastic drop in the number of priests over the past fifty years, in spite of half the world's Catholic parishes bereft of a resident pastor, remains off the table. Throughout his long papacy, John Paul II made it clear that the discipline of celibacy was nonnegotiable. He took pains to be perfectly clear that he did "not wish to leave any doubts in the mind of anyone regarding the church's firm will to maintain the law that demands perpetual and freely chosen celibacy for present and future candidates for priestly ordination in the Latin rite."[4] It is, he insisted, "the pearl of great price which is preferred to every other value no matter how great. . . ."[5]

In light of this state of affairs—growing sentiment for optional celibacy in the face of official church insistence that the law will be not be changed—it is likely that the Vatican is wary of *exceptions* to the rule of celibacy, though exceptions there are. For exceptions to a rule, if there are enough of them, tend to weaken its theoretical foundations. I think many church officials would prefer the present chapter to be titled, "Concessions to the Law of Celibacy," implying that while the exalted ideal of celibacy is clearly held and taught, some individual cases may merit exemptions. What follows here is a brief treatment of the exceptions to the rule as well as some flagrant flaunting of it.

It is well known that Orthodox Christianity, honoring a tradition rooted in the apostolic era, permits married men to be ordained. From their perspective, a married clergy is the norm and celibacy is the exception. Eastern churches in full communion with Rome, as noted in chapter three, have long permitted a married clergy. Nor would these truly Catholic churches see their traditions of a married clergy as exceptions or concessions. Yet, seen from the perspective of American Latin rite Catholics, whose numbers far exceed the populations of the six main Eastern rites, the married priests serving in these Eastern churches are regularly, though inaccurately, considered exceptions to the Latin rule of mandated celibacy.[6] Since the fathers of Vatican II pledged to honor and respect the traditions of these churches there seems no possibility of the Vatican trying to expand mandatory celibacy to include their clergy.[7] In 1929, when some U.S. bishops persuaded the Vatican to impose celibacy for Eastern rite priests living and ministering in Canada and the States, the anger and resentment that arose among them can still be felt today. Such an action would be unthinkable. It should be remembered, therefore, that for some Catholic seminarians, those preparing for the priesthood in non-Latin rites in Eastern Euro-Asia, optional celibacy is a reality, as long as they marry before they are ordained.

Are these married Catholic priests a kind of second class of priests? Are they to be assumed less holy, less pure, less dedicated to their ministry? Have they rejected the great pearl of the discipline of celibacy for the sacrament of marriage? Or has God called them to discipleship and holiness precisely through the sacraments of Orders and Matrimony? These Eastern rite priests, we might add, are the only Christians who are free, without the death of a spouse, to celebrate all seven of the church's sacraments.

A final consideration—one of Benedict XVI's major goals, if not *the* goal of his papacy, is the healing of the tragic separation in 1054 of Western Christianity from Eastern Orthodoxy. Since celibacy for Western clergy played a significant part in the schism, the issue will be key in the work for reunion.[8] If the church is indeed pledged to honor the tradition of married Eastern rite clergy, it can hardly expect Eastern Orthodoxy to require celibacy for its own clergy. At the same time, in light of the Western church's high rhetoric in praise of celibacy, would it be unthinkable for Vatican officials to strongly recommend celibacy for Orthodox priests? Should the schism be overcome soon, the celibacy issue for diocesan priests will have received major attention—and no doubt, dramatic change.

There are a number of Latin rite married priests currently ministering primarily in the United States and Great Britain. These men, as noted earlier, Episcopal priests and Protestant ministers, left their denominations to enter into full communion with the Latin-rite Catholic Church. They came with their wives and children and after appropriate retooling in seminaries, were ordained for ministry as Catholic priests. The motivating factor in their conversions appears to have been the ordination of women in their various denominations. Reports indicate that these married priests have generally been well received by their parishioners and Catholics in general.

What is of interest here is that so little is known about this phenomenon. We don't know the number of these married priests. Estimates range from 200 to 500 in the U.S. alone. We don't know the number who have received parish assignments and those who have been assigned as chaplains to church institutions. We don't know how their remuneration has been adjusted to meet their family expenses. Moreover, media coverage of their spiritual and religious journeys has been relatively scant, suggesting that they may have been encouraged to keep a low profile. If this is indeed the case, ecumenical sensitivity—not wanting to call unnecessary attention to clergy movement from one denomination to another—would explain the almost secretive character to this exception to the rule of celibacy. Also to be considered is the personal desire of at least some of these convert priests to avoid publicity. Many of these men, it appears, embraced Catholicism because of the Episcopal Church's decision to ordain women to the priesthood. Another factor might well be concern that widespread awareness of these exceptions might strengthen the case for optional celibacy.

It is hard to imagine a married priest sharing a rectory with a celibate priest. At the end of a tiring day, the celibate priest could hardly be blamed for twinges of envy as he says good night to his colleague. Especially for heterosexual priests, living in the same house with another man's wife could be problematic. It is highly unlikely that this situation would be allowed to develop—the dearth of priests itself argues against it—but its hypothetical character neverthe-less highlights the tensions that are likely to emerge when married and celibate priests serve in the same diocese.

Are celibacy's exceptions weakening the theological and spiritual foundations of obligatory celibacy? When a delegation of Canadian bishops requested permission to ordain married men to meet the pastoral needs of their people, it is reported that Cardinal Jozef Tomko, then head of the Congregation for the Evangelization of Peoples, said that any exception permitted in Canada "could not remain an exception," and would lead to an avalanche of similar requests from bishops in other countries.[9] But defenders of mandatory celibacy have a bigger concern than exceptions granted by the Holy See—the open disregard for celibacy in numerous parts of the world.

With notable exceptions, most of the calls for optional celibacy today come from Northern Europe, North America, Australia, Southwest Asia, Ireland, and England. Perhaps this reality manifests, although imperfectly, the kernel of truth contained in the over-generalized yet helpful distinction between Anglo-Saxon law and Latin or Mediterranean law. A law shaped by the Anglo-Saxon tradition understands compliance as the minimum. The church law requiring Catholics to celebrate Mass each Sunday, for example, is a fundamental and minimal duty of the believer. From this perspective, attending Mass on Sunday is minimally necessary for one's spiritual welfare, but going to Mass during the week, though not required by the law, is even better. From a Latin or Mediterranean perspective, law is commonly understood as the ideal to which all should strive.

Of course believers should go to Mass on Sunday. But this is understood as an ideal to be pursued. An Italian, so the story goes, was asked if he went to Mass each Sunday. "No," he said curtly. "I'm a Catholic, but not a fanatic."[10]

From the Anglo-Saxon perspective, minimal compliance with the law of celibacy is complete sexual continence in the state of consecrated singleness for the sake of the Kingdom. Lapses inevitably occur, but the law is understood as more than an ideal that may ultimately be beyond the reach of the priest. Compliance *is* expected. The Latin approach, on the other hand, may see the law of celibacy from a more relaxed, easygoing perspective. The reasoning goes something like this: Of course church law calls priests to be celibate, but this is the ideal. The urges of the body and the longings of the heart place this ideal out of reach, at least for many priests. Try to be celibate, but don't be fanatical about it. The latter understanding of law may explain why there are fewer calls for a change in mandated celibacy from priests in Spain and Italy than from priests in Northern Europe and North America.

This distinction came to mind when a colleague and I were leading a workshop for Irish missionaries. Mostly priests and sisters whose ministry took them to countries in Central and South America and to Africa, they spoke of the widespread lack of compliance to the law of obligatory celibacy—most of it undisguised, unhidden. Moreover, they claimed that the practice of clerical concubinage is commonly accepted by parishioners. Nor were bishops necessarily to be excluded from this practice.

Assuming these reports reflect a certain reality—the missionaries in our workshop were mature, faithful, seasoned sisters and priests—inevitable questions surface, both personal and institutional. Are the priests leading non-celibate lives conflicted, eager for mandatory celibacy to be overturned? Are they disturbed in conscience? Are they struggling, no matter how imperfectly, to be celibate or are they simply ignoring the obligation? How did the women in their lives affect their ministry, their spiritual lives? And for those priests with children, how did the experience of parenthood impact their personal and spiritual lives?

On a different level, how do we explain the church's apparent tolerance of this widespread disregard for the law of celibacy? Certainly Vatican officials are aware of the common non-compliance with mandated celibacy in these various locales. Bishops in private conversations will confirm the situation. Yet, inexplicably to the Anglo-Saxon mind, the missionaries in our workshop spoke of no ecclesiastical crackdown on this clerical state of affairs. Such church tolerance would be highly unlikely if a priest were living openly with a woman (or man) say, in the United States. Is the official church conceding that mandatory celibacy is simply not enforceable in certain societies and cultures? Is this a *de facto* recognition that there are two standards of celibacy? Celibacy's exceptions and the tragic scandal of clergy abuse of minors lead many to conclude that mandated celibacy is just not working. Is the Vatican's relative silence and inconsistent enforcement yet another manifestation of institutional denial?

The history of celibacy in the Catholic Church, we have seen, has always been troubled. This is so, in part at least, because human sexuality is so profoundly ambiguous and so profoundly complex. We believers are told to regard sexuality as a great gift from God that is in itself a manifestation of the divine presence, the longing for communion with the divine and all of reality. We are told at the same time that abstinence from sexual expression and a full erotic life is also a great gift—an even greater gift. We see authentic holiness and full human potential in men and women who have embraced celibacy for the Kingdom of heaven. We see authentic sanctity in the lives of married people whose genuine goodness and compassion reflect faithful, humble trust in the hidden presence of God. At the same time, the dark side of humanity lays bare sexuality's capacity to twist and ravage the human spirit.

Celibacy's troubles should not surprise. We compound these troubles, however, when we attempt to legislate that which is a free, mysterious gift given to relatively few human souls. All the exceptions, concessions, and dispensations that can possibly be granted simply postpone what is inevitable—a serious review of mandated celibacy.

CHAPTER FIVE

CELIBACY'S SHADOW

WHEN A WAY OF LIFE FITS, when an individual finds his or her life in harmony with one's destiny, that individual has come home—or better, has discovered the ease of being at home. There is a certain, more or less stable, congruity evident in such individuals. Their choices and callings merge and mix with their family histories and the "grace notes" of their past, those seemingly chance encounters with people and books and ideas that have shaped their lives. When reflected upon they see the vague outlines of what is commonly called *vocation*. These individuals have learned to listen to themselves—their inclinations, intuitions, the various "callings" that arise from their souls' centers. Here, quietly and gradually, they awaken to their gifts, to the gifts theologians call charisms. When in their company, their very presence seems to bless us. These men and women, we sense, are leading lives in harmony with their vocation, their calling, their destiny. Wherever they might be, they reflect the ease of being at home, with themselves, with others, with their world.

We all know such people. Most are married with children. Some are single men and women. Some are vowed religious and some are celibate priests. In spite of their human authenticity, in spite of their obvious at-home-ness, these men and women remain subject to human finitude and folly. Each has a shadow. Each deals with conflict, struggle, and tension. Each, from time to time, misses the mark. Though fundamentally "at home," they taste, nonetheless, the bitter herbs of alienation and estrangement. It is simply part of the human condition. Each of us, then, integrated or alienated, focused or confused, in harmony with God's plan or in a state of discord, sooner or later encounters our own shadow—that all too human capacity to play the fool.

And so it is with the major walks of life or lifestyles. Marriage has its shadow side: infidelity, spousal abuse, child neglect, divorce. The single life too: rootless-ness, loneliness and the pull to self-absorption. And, as we shall see below, so does celibacy, especially mandated celibacy imposed upon individuals not in possession of the charism.

Acknowledging the shadow inherent in each human being and in every walk of life, we turn now to the shadow side of obligatory or institutionalized celibacy.

Sitting alone late at night at his rectory's kitchen table, head in his hands, a priest heard himself say out load, "God takes no pleasure in this loneliness." Human suffering, we soon learn, is inevitable. While the ache of loneliness ranks rather low on the scale of human suffering, few if any escape its unsettling discomfort. Single people suffer loneliness; so do those who are married. Priests, no different from other men and women, know its bitter taste. God, I believe, takes no pleasure in any human suffering— especially suffering that is not necessary, not inherent to the human condition. And much of the emotional suffering linked to mandated celibacy is unnecessary. Nor does it seem that God takes pleasure in institutionalized celibacy. If God did, we would not have had the long, twelve-hundred-year tradition of married clergy in the Latin rite; we would not have the witness of two millennia of married clergy in the Orthodox communion and Eastern rite Catholic churches. We would not have listed in the canon of saints numerous married popes who with their wives established families and raised children.

Life, we know, is difficult and it should not unnecessarily be made more difficult. When the church presumes a charism in individuals presenting themselves for consideration as priests, it breaks the rhythm of grace. And like most things that are forced, demanding celibacy where the charism is not present unwittingly wounds not only the candidate but also puts the people to whom he will later minister as priest at risk. Grace simply refuses to be controlled—for in attempting to control grace we attempt to control God. When we enter these waters we face grave spiritual danger.

Peace, reverence, gratitude, hospitality, authenticity, and passion for life are some of the characteristics commonly found in men and women whose truth includes charismatic celibacy. When celibacy is imposed its shadow side, which includes the opposite of these characteristic virtues, readily comes to the surface.

The burden of obligatory celibacy easily disturbs the equilibrium of any individual not possessing its charism. Clearly, many clergy without the charism of celibacy have made their lives work. Their efforts often border on the

heroic. Their lives of prayer, their healthy friendships with
men and women, the support of family, and their fidelity
to ministry and the building up of the reign of God have
saturated their souls with a profound sense of meaning.
These priests bear witness to the transforming power of
the gospel. They radiate a peaceful calm and an abiding joy.
They are, I sometimes think, like the anonymous men and
women behind prison bars who nevertheless achieve true
liberty of soul. These priests are healthy, whole human be-
ings in spite of the imposed law of celibacy.

Others, it must be acknowledged, equally committed
to gospel service and lives of prayer, never find the whole-
ness of soul necessary for inner peace. Never quite at home
with themselves, their inner disquietude undermines their
peace of soul. As ministers of the church they may say the
right things and do the right things, but something doesn't
ring true. Not at home with themselves, they fail to be a
"beneficial presence." Not at home with themselves, they
fail to offer the hospitality at the core of the gospel.

When our life work is more or less in harmony with
our human aptitudes and our graced gifts, we come to
sense the mysterious workings of grace in our lives. We
are able to see beneath and beyond our achievements the
abiding work and presence of God's Spirit. Spontaneously
and without effort we give thanks. And our gratitude bears
fruit—an abiding reverence for all of creation, especially
for our brothers and sisters in the human family. However,
when our life's work, our vocation, assumes a charism we
do not possess, the consequent disharmony of soul easily
restricts our souls' capacity for gratitude and reverence.
Something's not right and like a pebble in our shoe the

distraction inhibits the self-forgetfulness that is essential for authentic gratitude and reverence and service.

Celibates "without charism" often fail to ring true. Not at home with themselves, their spiritual and psychological awkwardness keeps them from connecting with others, the very foundation skill of ministry. Priests in this category are especially susceptible to the pseudo-identity found in clericalism.[1] Here priests over-identify with their public persona making authentic relating nearly impossible. Cloaked in the mantel of ecclesiastical manners and propriety, they present themselves as not quite real—and not quite in touch. Often their artificial culture depletes their creativity and passion for life. Moreover, their relationships tend to be superficial and formal or strained and immature. Not surprisingly, their preaching is often didactic and dry. Sooner or later these shadow forces lead to compensatory behaviors and attitudes of privilege and power.

Psychotherapists who work with priests commonly remark that unrecognized anger is a common issue. Simmering frustrations rooted in the lack of appropriate control of the more foundational aspects of their lives—place of work, dress, sexuality—seem to be factors here. Perhaps compensating for this lack of personal control, some priests show high need for control in their ministries. Moreover, obsessive-compulsive traits are common in celibate clergy.

These shadow dimensions to mandated celibacy are surely of the garden-variety type. We find them wherever people willfully strive to be something they are not suited for by temperament, aptitude, and grace. In spite of the relative simplicity of the celibate life compared to the challenges of marriage, children, and mortgage, for many priests called to ordained ministry but not to celibacy, the challenges of ministry and adulthood are greatly intensified—and they and their ministry suffer. But mandated celibacy casts a far darker shadow in the lives of some priests, a shadow that has and continues to scar parishioners both young and old.

When individuals declare themselves, by choice or necessity, to be off limits, to be out of the game, so to speak, their sexual appeal in many cases increases. From the days of the vestal virgins to the troubadours' lyrical praise of courtly love to our secular society's obsession with sex, celibacy's alchemy reveals a formula proven to be both alluring and seductive. What is not available has the potential to awaken interest and even desire. In the case of celibate priests, when the laity's understanding of their spiritual power to consecrate bread and wine into the body and blood of Christ and to forgive sin is added to the formula, the attraction meter rises considerably. Add to this mix the compassion, the gift for attention, and the generosity of soul evident in the lives of many priests, and one discovers a corps of men with considerable personal appeal—regardless of their physical attractiveness.

A wealth of anecdotal evidence supports the allure and attraction celibate priests hold for numerous women. Diocesan personnel files and archives tell stories of priests involved with both single and married women. Not infrequently, children are conceived—and sometimes aborted. Jane Anderson, an Australian anthropologist, studied the romantic and sexual involvement of fifty priests.[2] Her report, based on interviews over a nine year period with straight and gay priests, captures the emotional and spiritual struggles of the men in question and, by inference, the priests' partners. Some, obviously conflicted, acknowledge feelings of guilt and compromised integrity. Others, however, insist they have found the spiritual and human fulfillment they had longed for throughout their priesthood. Many report little if any guilt. Two explanations come to mind. The priests see the law of mandated celibacy as unjust and, therefore, not binding, or they acknowledge the ideal of the law (the Mediterranean or Latin approach to law discussed earlier) as something, someday, they hope to attain. Others will argue that they have simply dulled their consciences.

Other celibate relationships, while not explicitly sexual, lead to deep emotional involvement and commitment. Some are celebrated in the annals of our spiritual tradition as profoundly graced friendships—St. Francis and St. Clair, Jordan of Saxony (the second master of the Dominican Order) and Diana d'Andalo (the first Domincan prioress), Pope Pius XII and Sr. Pasqualina come to mind. Clearly, however, not all celibate friendships are so blessed. There are other affairs of the heart that reveal immaturity and crass exploitation. In the latter case, the priest may be simultaneously involved with more than one woman or man. Should the priest end the relationship, citing his love of the priesthood and his calling to ministry, the emotional suffering of his partner can be shattering.

While numerous clergy relationships embody the shadow side of celibacy, there remain countless celibate friendships that appear to be profoundly healthy and both humanly and spiritually fulfilling. Open to misunderstanding and preemptive judgment, these friendships are, more often than not, sustained with considerable discretion.

There is no need here to review the well-documented tragic betrayal of the clergy abuse scandal. While the scandal's shadow continues to expand, Catholics have become almost numbed to the seeming endless accounts of unimaginable suffering inflicted on thousands of children and youth by Catholic priests and bishops. Reports continue to surface more than twenty-five years after the *National Catholic Reporter* first broke the story of a scandal that has led to the greatest crisis the U.S. Catholic Church has ever faced. Because of the scandal, conservative, moderate, and progressive Catholics have been awakened as if from a centuries-old adolescent sleep. To the consternation of many church authorities, they now expect to be treated as adult disciples entitled to know why their bishops were so reluctant to honestly address the issue and why they permitted—by moving abuser priests from parish to parish— untold numbers of youngsters to be included among the victims of clergy abusers. Now, no longer suffering from any illusions, they insist on knowing how and where their church contributions are being spent. They are convinced that accountability and transparency are their right and not a concession of church authorities.

The church in North America will never be quite the same. Still, caution is necessary in linking the abuse scandal to the law requiring celibacy for priests of the Latin rite. Defenders of mandatory celibacy are quick to point out that most child molesters are married men. Of course. The population of married men far surpasses the population of celibate priests. The real question is one of proportionality. Does the percentage of married men who abuse children and teen-aged minors exceed the percentage of priests who do so? Since most abusers of minors, clergy and non-clergy, are never found out, the question may never be satisfactorily answered. Nevertheless, studies linked to the National Review Board Report find that in numerous U.S. dioceses roughly eight to ten percent of their priests have had credible accusations brought against them. Knowing these figures to be conservative—most incidents of child abuse go unreported—Catholics wonder just what is going on.

Is it possible that obligatory celibacy unwittingly fosters psycho-sexual immaturity among seminarians and priests? And that this immaturity in turn fosters a truncated, repressed sexual development among these same men? Individuals coping with underdeveloped sexual and emotional maturation find teens and children far less threatening objects of sexual attraction. Celibate, intimate friendships and relationships with peers are likely to be all too threatening for emotionally immature adults—and priests. It appears the National Review Board appointed by Bishop Wilton Gregory in 2002 thinks so. They conclude that "There can be no doubt that while it is a gift for some, celibacy is a terrible burden for others, resulting in loneliness, alcohol and drug abuse, and improper sexual conduct . . . that demands further study."[3]

Finally, a brief look to the church's past. Mandated celibacy for Latin rite priests, as noted earlier, became universal law at the Second Lateran Council in 1139. It has been enforced, unevenly and often callously, for the last nine centuries of the church's two-millennia-plus history. And the darkest, longest shadows of illicit sexual indulgence were cast by many of the Renaissance popes and large numbers of their clergy. Rivaling the corruption of the tenth-century papacy, the Renaissance popes gave substance and form to the church's "moral dark ages." While none of the Renaissance popes have been considered worthy of sainthood and most were tainted with nepotism, two were notorious for their egregious disregard for the law of obligatory celibacy.

Alexander VI, pope from 1492 to 1503, is infamous for a pontificate "marked by nepotism, greed, and unbridled sensuality."[4] The nephew of Pope Callistus III, he was named a cardinal by his uncle when only in his mid twenties. A year after being appointed to the College of Cardinals, his uncle named him vice-chancellor of the Holy See, a position that allowed him to amass huge sums of money. Both as a cardinal and as pope, Alexander had little regard for mandated celibacy and his promise following his election as pope to reform the college of cardinals of the vice of simony—the buying or selling of ecclesiastical appointments, preferments, or pardons—was soon abandoned. Both before and after his election as pope, Alexander, officially celibate, fathered numerous children. There appears little remorse of conscience, little struggle to remain celibate—and apparently no thought of changing the law of mandated celibacy. Was this a manifestation of the shadow side of the Latin approach to law?

Like many of the Renaissance popes, Julius III (pope from 1550 to 1555) was fond of hunting, feasting, lavish entertainment, and furthering the interests of his family. His fidelity to celibacy is highly questionable. Scandal erupted when Julius, smitten by a fifteen-year-old boy he encountered on the streets of Parma, named the boy a cardinal and then Secretary of State—while still in his teens. Not surprisingly, the attitude of many of the lower clergy of the period concerning celibacy reflected the example of Alexander and Julius.

As if to counter the general disregard for celibacy among the higher and lower clergy, great-souled individuals rose up at the same time to bear witness to charismatic celibacy and to strengthen a church reeling from the Reformation. St. Ignatius of Loyola founded the Jesuits in 1534 followed by St. Philip Neri's Oratorians, St. Angela Merici's Ursulines, and later by St. Vincent de Paul's Vincentians and St. Louise de Marillac's Sisters of Charity, among numerous other religious congregations committed to celibacy and service.

The roots of clerical infidelity and immorality during the Renaissance reach beyond mandated celibacy, of course, but the law of celibacy should not be dismissed as a shaping factor during these "moral dark ages." While the period between 1400 and 1600 may be the nadir of clerical immorality, it is by no means the only historical period where clergy not graced with the charism of celibacy, yet required to live it, betrayed the gospel, scandalized the faithful, and tragically assaulted the innocence and faith of the most vulnerable and defenseless of believers.

CHAPTER SIX

CELIBACY AND HOMOSEXUALITY

IN LATE WINTER OF 2000, while president-rector of Cleveland's Saint Mary Seminary, I called attention to the disproportionately high numbers of gay seminarians and priests.[1] More than a decade earlier theologian Richard McBrien and sociologist Andrew Greeley had addressed the issue in prominent Catholic publications.[2] Vehement, almost hysterical denials were leveled at the three of us. This, in spite of broad agreement among seminary rectors and faculties, as well as bishops with extensive experience in seminary formation that there were and are large numbers of homosexually oriented men in the priesthood and in our seminaries. Indeed, some of the best and brightest of our seminarians, priests, and bishops are gay. Like their straight brothers in ministry, most strive—and sometimes struggle—to lead chaste and holy lives. And like their straight brothers, some fail miserably—including tragic, criminal assaults against minors and children that have tumbled the U.S. Catholic Church into its worst crisis ever. Elsewhere, I have explored the implications of this reality from the perspective of seminary culture and formation, the critical drop in the number of seminarians, and the growing awareness that the priesthood is or is becoming a "gay profession."[3]

The denial has softened if not collapsed. Without question, the clergy abuse scandal has contributed greatly to the growing awareness of large numbers of gay clergy. Some conservative Catholics see a direct causal link between gay priests and bishops and the abuse scandal. They point out that by a wide margin, most of the victims of clergy abuse of minors have been teenage boys. Get rid of the gays in the clergy, they propose, and you will get rid of the abuse scandal. Most Catholics, I suspect, believe that sexual orientation, while not a cause of abuse in itself, is nonetheless a factor that must be considered.

Much of the consideration, unfortunately, has been profoundly problematic. In late November of 2005, the Vatican Congregation for Catholic Education issued an "Instruction," with the pope's approval, directing bishops, seminary rectors, and religious superiors not to admit a candidate to seminary formation who "practices homosexuality, presents deep-seated homosexual tendencies or supports the so-called 'gay culture.'"[4]

Implementation of the Instruction is a moral minefield. A gay candidate who sincerely believes God is calling him to priesthood must discern if his homoerotic tendencies are, in the language of the Instruction, an "expression of a transitory problem" or "deep-seated homosexual tendencies." Nor can a gay candidate decide "not to tell" seminary authorities for, the Instruction declares, "It would be gravely dishonest for a candidate to hide his own homosexuality in order to proceed, despite everything, toward ordination." Moreover, while most adults discover their sexual identity early on in childhood or at least by their adolescent years, some individuals become clear about their orientation only in their middle years. Furthermore, there is no clear, reliable test to determine sexual orientation. In spite of psychological procedures designed to identify orientation, it comes down to an individual's self-declaration. And how are seminary officials to measure "deep-rooted homosexual tendencies" from tendencies that are not deep-rooted? And is it not possible that a seminary candidate with deep-rooted homosexual tendencies may be at the same time emotionally and affectively mature and capable of effective pastoral and spiritual leadership?

Ironically, the Vatican Instruction is being implemented in numerous cases by bishops, seminary rectors, and religious superiors who are gay themselves. The perceived hypocrisy in such situations is not lost on large numbers of the laity and clergy, regardless of their orientation. It is not surprising, then, that the cover letter accompanying the Instruction directed bishops not to appoint gay priests as seminary rectors or gay men to seminary faculty positions. Finally, the document raised fears in some church circles that angry, celibate gay priests, frustrated with the incongruity if not hypocrisy of gay bishops and rectors implementing the Instruction, would "out" gay bishops and other highly placed churchmen.

The charged feelings surrounding the issue of gay priests, bishops, and seminarians will only be dissipated when the reality of homosexuals in the ranks of the clergy is dealt with openly, compassionately, and with wisdom. The major obstacle to such a response by church officials is the Vatican's insistence that same-sex attraction is objectively disordered. Perhaps only when openly gay believers who have led lives of irreproachable moral integrity and holiness are added to the canon of saints will the moral cloud hanging over the heads of gay laity and clergy be lifted.

In the meantime, the impact of the Instruction on seminary enrollments will likely be to shrink the already drastically reduced pool of seminarians—and deepen the Eucharistic crisis steadily spreading throughout the church.

Our focus here, however, remains on mandated celibacy and homosexual priests. Why, it is logical to ask, would a gay believer want to be a celibate priest? As officials of the church, priests are charged with the promulgation of church teaching and with presenting it in as compelling a manner as possible. Pastorally, they are to uphold this teaching even when it is challenged or rebuffed. Gay priests find themselves in a position where they are expected to teach clearly that a homosexual orientation is intrinsically and objectively disordered. They may not feel that their own orientation is flawed, unnatural, sick, or disordered, but they are expected to hold publicly that it is abnormal and disordered. They are further charged to instruct gay people that their orientation calls them to lives of perfect sexual continence—as the church calls all who are unmarried to perfect sexual continence. For, according to church teaching, all deliberate sexual desires and behaviors outside of married love open to the conception of children are objectively wrong and mortally sinful. Gay priests, then, are likely to encounter a kind of existential "conflict of interest." Often, they report, their personal and pastoral experience convinces them that their orientation is not objectively disordered—that it is not perverse.

Reconciling their personal and pastoral experience with official church teaching was made more difficult in 2002 when Vatican spokesperson, Joaquin Navarro-Valls, questioned the validity of gay priests' ordination. Later the same year, a priest assigned to the Vatican, Andrew Baker, argued that gay men were inherently unsuited for the priesthood because they were inclined to "substance abuse, sexual addiction, and depression."[5]

So why might gay believers be drawn to the priesthood? Some acknowledge that the suspicion they were gay filled them with terror and even disgust. Aware of the church's teaching that a same-sex orientation is objectively disordered, the very celibacy of the priesthood was appealing. They believed they might be able to put their sexuality "on the shelf," so to speak. As celibates, they imagined—and hoped—there would be no need to deal with the issue. Sexual orientation, after all, is commonly thought to be a moot question for the celibate. Or so it might seem. But coming to terms with one's orientation, whether straight or gay, is critical to the formation of a healthy and integrated personality. Attempts to put sexuality "on the shelf" or to deny or repress its energy and power prove, sooner or later, to backfire. To the extent that sexuality remains unintegrated into an individual's personality and psychic life, it remains potentially dangerous, waiting to erupt in destructive ways to both the individual and others. Moreover, there is no real spiritual maturation or emotional maturation without a healthy sense of one's sexuality and orientation. Only when spiritually and emotionally mature are we capable of understanding the urgent longings of the heart—and see that sexual energy

is ultimately a sacrament of our deepest desire—communion with God and all of creation.

Another reason why gay individuals are drawn to the
priesthood is the great irony and paradox of the church—
it is both and at the same time "modern and yet medieval, ascetic and yet sumptuous, spiritual and yet sensual,
chaste and yet erotic, homophobic and yet homoerotic
. . . ."[6] No one has better captured this paradox than Ellis
Hanson in his book, *Decadence and Catholicism*. While
the focus of the quote that follows is on gay priests who
are fascinated with young boys, his analysis is nonetheless
illuminating for why gay men are drawn to the priesthood
in spite of the church's teaching that same sex attraction is
objectively disordered.

"I have often been asked . . . why a gay man or a
lover of boys would become a priest. The motives are so
numerous, however, that the real question ought to be why
straight men become priests. Beyond faith, which I gather
to be the primary appeal, since the priesthood would be
unbearable without it, there are other motivations for
men of a certain inclination: the effeminized pastoral persona, the pleasures of ritual, [until recently] public trust
and respect, freedom from the social pressure to marry,
opportunity for intimacy with boys, passionate friendship
and cohabitation with likeminded men and a discipline for
coping with sexual shame and guilt."[7]

From the perspective of human dynamics, Hanson, I
believe, has hit the mark. From a theological perspective,
however, his analysis is minimally helpful. Gay men are
drawn to the priesthood, in most instances, I believe, because they believe they have received a calling to ordained

ministry—in other words, they believe they have a vocation, a charism to ministry as priests. And some gay men
believe they are called to celibate chastity—in other words,
they believe they have the charism, the grace of celibacy.
Most, however, aware of no such gift, strive mightily along
side their straight brothers to lead celibate lives.

Struggling to be men of integrity, some gay priests,
like thousands of their straight brothers who have left active ministry to marry, have also left convinced that their
need for human and sexual intimacy left them no alternative. Many of these men believed they were indeed called to
priesthood, but not to lives of celibate continence. Often they
are judged more harshly than priests who leave to marry.
Others find the celibate priesthood a comfortable place to
live out their sexual denial and repression. Still others, like
some straight priests, find the celibate priesthood the perfect cover (until recently) for complete sexual fulfillment.

From time to time I am asked the question, "Do you think
it is easier for straight or gay priests to lead lives of celibate chastity?" Ultimately unanswerable, the question
appears to be prompted by the realization that authentic
celibate living for most priests and religious is aided and
sustained by and through authentic, intimate, non-sexual
friendships with both men and women of one's own age
cohort. For straight priests this would include friendships
with women; for the gay priest, friendships with men.
Now healthy friendships have a certain public character
to them. Friends, at least from time to time, are seen in
public—in coffee houses, restaurants, the theater. Often
their wider circle of friends as well as their families know

of their significant friendships. Instinctively, we suspect something is wrong if a friendship is characterized by secrecy and discretion.

A gay priest who is blessed with a mature, intimate, and celibate friendship with another priest or layman moves easily in the public sphere of life. Priests, after all, are meant to find friendship with other men. He spends his day off in the company of a particular male friend. He can vacation with him, travel with him, eat out with him. He is comfortable being seen in his presence. These friendships, assuming they are celibate, are sources of authentic human and spiritual joy. When both friends are priests, they draw upon their shared seminary years, the stories and humor that have their own bonding power. Their common interest in liturgy, Scripture, literature, and the arts, not to mention church gossip, regularly lead to lively conversation and true fraternity. While there is a certain risk to such intimate friendships, the greater risk, I'm convinced, is to attempt to lead a celibate life, whether gay or straight, that eschews meaningful and close relationships.

From a social, public arena point of view, it is likely easier for a gay priest to sustain and enjoy a close, intimate friendship with another man—and theoretically, at least, to lead a healthy, life-giving, celibate life.

Straight priests, on the other hand, blessed with a close, intimate, yet celibate friendship with a woman navigate a different social terrain. The long-established expectation is that priests will be seen in the company of other priests or in the company of men—and until recently, young men, even boys. A certain awkwardness still remains when a priest is seen in public with a woman. Social expectations, then, tend to make priest-woman friendships, no matter how authentic, graced, and celibate, more difficult to negotiate. To the extent that this is true, celibacy for the straight priest may prove more difficult at times than for the gay priest.

For the heterosexually oriented priest struggling with the inherent loneliness of celibacy, the apparent social freedom he sees gay priests enjoying may lead to feelings of envy. Some will acknowledge, when the company can be trusted, that there already exists optional celibacy—for the gay priest. For only the personal integrity of the gay priest, his spiritual and emotional maturity, keeps him from, rather easily, leading a sexually active life.

Gay or straight, the challenge to lead a healthy, creative celibate life is greatly enhanced by the life-giving gift of close, personal, celibate friendship. We have not always thought so. For centuries, seminary faculty warned seminarians to forgo "particular friendships" with other seminarians. The unstated reason behind this rule was fear of homosexual liaisons. Seminarians were expected, of course, not to date while home on vacation nor were they to have close friends who were women. Only a generation ago, a seminarian's mail was opened and his phone calls restricted. God, his family, and the all-male community of seminary colleagues were judged to be sufficient for his emotional and spiritual development both as a priest and a human being. Friendship, whether with a man or a woman, was perceived in these pre-Vatican II years to be the great danger to a celibate life. And, it appears, in some seminaries it still is.

Without human intimacy the healthiest of vocations becomes strained and often twisted.[8] The tragic scandal of priests and bishops abusing minors, I believe, has underscored this reality. Deep, committed friendships are not without their dangers for celibate priests. The greater danger, by far, is for priests to think they are not like the rest of men.

In a previous book, I addressed the issue of celibate loving. It speaks, I believe, to both gay and straight celibate relationships. "One of the untold stories of the priesthood at the close of the twentieth century is the large number of life-giving, joyful, loving friendships between celibate priests and their committed friends. Both straight and gay priests have sustained celibate relationships of real grace and depth. From time to time mistakes have been made—some proving to be tragic. And from time to time the struggle to keep a friendship celibate may be intense. Only prudence, honesty, and above all, God's grace can nurture celibate friends into true soul-mates. . . . Priests gifted with authentic celibate relationships often discover a transformation of soul, a compassion and strength previously unknown to them. In spite of the suffering that inevitably touches all human love and friendship, priests blessed with celibate, loving intimacy give thanks for the wonder of it all. In the process, they believe they have grown as men of God, as men of the church."[9]

CHAPTER SEVEN

CELIBACY AS POWER

Pow·er, n. the ability or capacity to perform or act effectively; the ability or official capacity to exercise control; authority.

POWER, LIKE CELIBACY, carries its own erotic energy. I remember reading that Henry Kissinger believed he was one of the sexiest men in Washington. Not because of his good looks (few would call him handsome) or his engaging personality (he often looked to me as if he were about to doze off) or his great intellect, but because he was one of the most powerful players in Washington—and therefore one of the most powerful figures in the world. Power, even more so than celibacy, more than interests us, it fascinates us. For many, the kind of political power exercised by Kissinger and other top governmental figures, especially heads of state, is the ultimate power. The power of wealth, in contrast, provides the trappings of power—million-dollar homes, luxury cars, exotic vacations, social status—but the power to govern, to command and control, and to directly shape economic and social policies remains, in secular societies at least, the epitome of power.

Before the modern era it was the power of the hierarchic church that was considered ultimate, for the church was perceived as the arbiter of salvation with powers to both grant forgiveness from sin and to excommunicate. Powers linked with an individual's personal salvation or damnation are indeed ultimate to the believer. Moreover, some medieval popes, for example Boniface VIII, claimed absolute, universal sovereignty, both spiritual *and* temporal.[1] It was with this kind of power in mind that Lord Acton uttered his chilling declaration that power corrupts and that absolute power corrupts absolutely.

Our concern here is, for the most part, with a different kind of power. It is best to see it as attendant power for celibacy's power is essentially derivative. While both personal and social in nature, the power associated with celibacy finds its source in ecclesiastical and spiritual power. It remains, nonetheless, as exhilarating, perplexing, dangerous, and ambiguous as any other kind of power.

After ordination, at least since the last of the married popes (Hadrian II, 867–872), the defining characteristic of ecclesiastical power has and continues to be celibacy. From the end of the first millennium, popes, bishops, and priests of the Western church, influenced by a dualistic neo-Platonism, the example of the Desert Fathers, and the rise of monasticism, more and more came to see celibacy as fitting for their clerical state. And by the middle of the twelfth century it was obligatory. Soon the power of ecclesiastical office merged with the power of clerical celibacy. It was deemed, by most clergy and laity, fitting and appropriate that those who spoke for God and for God's church be celibate. Celibacy was now woven into the very fabric of clerical cloth—and became the badge of ecclesiastical status and power.

Now, after nine centuries of mandated celibacy which linked church authority and leadership with unmarried clerics, the Catholic imagination is awakening to new possibilities rooted in the church's ancient tradition. The Second Vatican Council's affirmation of human sexuality, the emergence of Catholic feminism, the dearth of priestly vocations, and the clergy abuse scandals have raised serious questions about the wisdom of mandated celibacy. Yet, it continues to be staunchly defended by the highest church authority. Why?

From an administrative point of view, and here we are talking power, mandated celibacy is arguably the linchpin of the ecclesiastical system. No one is more controlled than when his or her sexuality is controlled. Control another's sexuality, and you control his center of vitality, the core of his identity and integrity. Just as boarding schools attempt to control the sexuality of adolescent boys and girls, the institutional church attempts to control the sexuality of its priests. And many priests take on the resentment and immaturity of boarded adolescents. They can become obsessed with that which is forbidden—waiting for vacations and other opportunities to break out and experiment.

Experienced headmasters tend to treat their students as quasi-adults with clear boundaries demarking what is permitted and what is forbidden. Discipline is strictly enforced and comportment appropriately rewarded. Good intentions notwithstanding, most boarding schools cannot escape a hothouse environment. Emotionally and psychologically, mandatory celibacy places priests in the hothouse environment of the boarding school. It's difficult to live as an adult there, and resentments deepen. Moreover, it's difficult for a priest, in the hothouse of clerical culture, to relate to his bishop as another adult rather than as a headmaster.

Episcopal power, from this perspective, is controlling rather than liberating. It may be exercised with all the good intentions of a wise and caring headmaster, but both bishop and priest remain, at least on one level, less than fully adult. Such is the case when power is exercised as power *over* rather than power *for*. Power *over* is the kind of power used by adults to control the behavior of their children. When children become adults, however, a different model of authority is employed. Instead of commanding and controlling, parents exercise influential power, grounded in discourse and persuasion, for the well-being and liberation of their adult children. Here, everything depends on the integrity and authenticity of the parents. Modeling becomes as important as advising, counseling, and exhortation. To say to an adult child, "I forbid you . . . ," no longer works.

The same is true for the exercise of church power. Without denying the necessity, from time to time, for church officials to exercise power *over*, church authority is fundamentally an exercise of power *for* the liberation and maturation in grace of adult believers. It is power *for* the necessary order to fulfill the church's mission—to bring to the world the liberating and saving grace of Jesus the Christ in the power of the Holy Spirit. It should be less concerned with propositional statements of doctrine, as necessary and important as they are, than with the relational life of faith in God as revealed in Christ and his gospel—from which propositional teachings flow. Here, modeling is even more important than advising, counseling, and exhortation. Here, too, everything depends on integrity and authenticity. Ecclesial power exercised as command and control authority no longer works for thoughtful, reflective, adult believers. It may have in earlier eras when the feudal structure of the institutional church worked—but it doesn't today.

Clearly, celibacy has many administrative advantages. Changing the assignment of a celibate priest, for example, is far less complicated than moving a married priest from one parish to another. There is no wife to consult, no change of schools for children, and most often no mortgage to be negotiated. The same relative ease accompanies the move of a bishop from one diocese to another. Calling celibate priests and bishops to serve in Vatican curial positions is likewise facilitated when those promoted are celibate.

The power of a bishop to assign clergy with relative ease and efficiency pales, however, when compared to the power a bishop holds over the personal lives of his priests. Not only does a bishop control the assignments and places of ministry of his priests, he has immediate power over their advancement—their careers—as churchmen. Here the power to advance within church structures is linked to obedience and loyalty. Both the power dynamic and the emotional/psychological dynamic between bishop and priest would be noticeably different absent mandatory celibacy.

It is celibacy, more than holy orders, that establishes the pseudo-paternal and familial bond between a priest and his bishop.[2] And it is celibacy that gives tone and nuance to clerical culture's ethereal reality of mystique, mystery, and privilege. While clericalism, the perversion of gospel service and ministry, can be found among Orthodox, married priests, it remains the bane of Western, non-married clergy—and is reinforced by institutional celibacy.[3]

The power to play the "clerical game" emerges from understanding how power is gained and exercised in the celibate, feudal world of the church. Beyond a certain level of talent, the rules are few but demanding: docility, loyalty, and external compliance with each and every church policy and directive, no matter how distant these may be from doctrine and dogma. Priests eager to get in the game embrace celibacy without question. It is their key to ecclesiastical advancement. The price that is paid, however, diminishes the priest's power to imagine and inspire, key factors in effective preaching and spiritual leadership.

Most priests, I believe, negotiate the power trap rather well. Freed from the power dynamics of ecclesiastical careerism, they tend to be, in growing numbers, both men of the church and their own men. They use their power wisely and effectively, understanding that they are priests empowered by God's grace and their God-given gifts and talents for ministry. Building on a power bestowed, their ministry remains fundamentally service rather than control. When they speak, their words are effective, that is, powerful, communicating a presence that is authoritative without being authoritarian. The ministry of these men of the church is consistently liberating rather than controlling and encouraging rather than condemning.

When charismatic celibacy coincides with institutional celibacy, as it clearly does in the lives of numerous priests, we see a liberation of soul, an empowerment of spirit, and the joy that comes from fidelity to one's gifts. Charismatic celibates, as we have seen, have "an existential inability to do otherwise." And because they are at home with their destiny and vocation, they reflect the *joy of celibacy*. Here, perhaps, is celibacy's greatest power—bearing joyful witness to the unseen order of grace, to the mystery of selfless love, to the transcendent, saving powers of the God we cannot see.

Charismatic celibacy, then, is liberating, authoritative, and joyful. In other words, it is packed with power. It remains attractive and fascinating because it is *real*. And because its reality is grounded in the ultimate reality of the divine, it is also sacramental. It is in this sense that we speak of celibacy as a great gift to the church and to the world—a great sign of the subtext of grace permeating the human story.

When mandatory celibacy, however, does not coincide with charismatic celibacy, it disempowers rather than empowers. Ideally, celibacy is meant to serve the vitality of the church and its mission. Mandated celibacy, to the contrary, drains the psychic energy of the priest not in possession of the charism. Often distracted by the struggle to remain faithful to celibate chastity, the relative ease of soul and personality that fosters effective and creative ministry is painfully absent. Coping with the inflated loneliness of obligatory celibacy, priests instinctively tend to various compensations, some innocent and harmless enough, others often destructive and even lethal.

Harry Byrne, a retired priest of the archdiocese of New York, reflected on the distractions and compensations fostered by mandated celibacy: "Now at age eighty-three, after fifty-nine years of a happy and exciting priesthood, my early questioning of celibacy has been confirmed. Rather than an enhancement, celibacy has been more of a distraction. Unmarried, the priest ideally can give more of himself and his time to ministry, but it does not always work out that way. Compensations easily insinuate themselves—golf, tennis, bridge, social activities, hobbies—and make disproportionate demands on the time and energy said to derive from celibacy. Without a high-octane spiritual life, other less acceptable activities can come into play: drinking, race tracks, casinos. As a form of asceticism, celibacy's heroic demands are more at home with a hermit in the desert or a monk in the monastery than with a priest ministering in today's highly charged sexual atmosphere."[4]

Sadly, it is not uncommon to find middle-aged celibate priests preoccupied with an adolescent curiosity about sex that borders on obsession. Often fixated in their psychosexual development at the adolescent stage, their sexual interest mirrors their arrested maturation. These priests find themselves drawn to attractive teenagers. The dangers associated with such truncated emotional and sexual maturation have been made painfully clear with the sexual abuse scandals that erupted in the last decades of the twentieth century.

Sensing the absence of full adulthood that should correspond to their chronological age, some celibate priests compensate for their diminished personal power with a surprising preoccupation with money. Money's power fills up their inner emptiness and soothes the anxiety that accompanies disempowerment. My hunch is that there are more priest-millionaires or near-millionaires in the U. S. than we might believe. Mostly they come by their money through intelligent investments in securities augmented by frugal living and disciplined saving, and sometimes by silent partnerships in various businesses. Some wealthy priests have simply benefited from family inheritances. Others, sadly, have exploited the feudal dominion they exercise over parish finances in spite of diocesan policies and parish finance council oversight designed to safeguard fiscal integrity.

Priests, like most people, are as secretive about money as they are about sex. While no research, to my knowledge, has been focused on the psychology of high-income clergy, I suspect the wealthy priest phenomenon is more driven by the need for a sense of autonomy than by simple greed. Wealthy priests almost invariably tend to lead inconspicuous and simple lifestyles. It appears their interest in money is more an emotional comfort and a kind of armor against their powerlessness than a desire for material things and the vaunted good life of Western capitalism.

While money may be a compensation for the perceived powerlessness of some priests, more than a few pastors, as if reacting to their status as clerical vassals to the lord bishop, act with unbridled power in the fiefdoms of their own parishes. These men rule their staffs as an aloof employer and mistrust the ecclesial values of cooperation and collegiality. Often sexually repressed and without the joy of healthy, close friendships with peers, they distract themselves from their solitary existence by their own brand of command and control.

In spite of celibacy's ability to disempower—keeping adult men in more or less of an adolescent state—rather than empower, there is evidence that the clergy are coming of age. From coast to coast, more and more presbyterates (the diocesan and religious order priests serving in a given diocese) are taking their pastoral experience seriously and speaking with strength and conviction about the structural renewal and reform necessary for the vitality of the church. Overcoming the reticence and docility of centuries of clerical conditioning, they are finding their voice.

Countering the dark shadows cast by the clergy abuse scandals, these priests are choosing to stand in the light and speak as mature believers who have firsthand experience of the joys and sorrows, the hopes and fears, the successes and failures of their parishioners. Among themselves, these priests acknowledge their own joys and sorrows, their own hopes and fears, their own successes and failures. As they do so, the power that emerges is simply the power of the gospel, the power of the Spirit—and the very authority of Jesus the Christ.

CHAPTER EIGHT

CELIBACY AS OPPRESSION

Op·pres·sion, n. the act of oppressing; the imposition of unreasonable burdens; the state of being oppressed or overburdened.

NO ONE FORCES A MAN to be ordained. Pressure is sometimes felt from a seminarian's mother, but he stands before the ordaining bishop as an adult having moved through a seminary formation program that has emphasized again and again the rigors of the priesthood—especially the responsibilities and challenges associated with celibacy. He is asked formally and ritually to declare his freedom in accepting the responsibilities of priesthood including the obligation to lead a chaste, celibate life of sexual continence (the redundancy here is intentional). An adult believer, educated and formed during years of seminary training, declaring publicly his readiness to accept ordination, and knowing the obligations inherent in celibacy, he kneels while hands are imposed and rises a priest forever. Oppression? Hardly, at least at first glance.

A second look is revealing. Most diocesan priests, and many religious order priests as well, speak of the "priesthood package."[1] They report feeling called to priesthood, a priesthood that for almost a millennium has included

celibacy. The felt call to priesthood was strong and enduring and while many, if not most, diocesan priests did not
experience a similar enduring call to celibacy, their vocation to holy orders overrode any reservations about celibacy. You simply "couldn't have one without the other."
Echoes of this sentiment were heard earlier in the voices
of Bishop John Crowley and Monsignor Harry Byrne.[2]
In today's post-Vatican II world, especially among the
well educated peoples of Euro-America, Catholics know
the history of their church—and its tradition of a married clergy for more than eleven hundred years. They
understand more clearly than ever what is essential to the
priesthood and what is not.

For a priest blessed with the charism, celibacy is liberating.
What would be oppressive for such a priest would be to
insist that he marry—or to pressure him to marry. Since
charisms can't be legislated by their very nature, the incongruity of attempts to do so becomes ludicrously clear
when we draw out the implications of this hypothetical
situation. Imagine, then, a church law requiring seminarians to marry before they can be ordained.[3] Most might
feel called to marriage as well as to priesthood. And where
there is a call from God, one can assume the charism to
live out that call. But for seminarians called to both celibacy and priesthood, the requirement to marry would
indeed be oppressive because they would not enjoy the
charism of marriage. Here it is as if the church is saying
to the seminarian, "Even though you may not feel called
to marriage, God will give you the grace to lead a faithful,
happy married life. God will bless you with the charism of

marriage." In this imagined scenario, the church would be presumptive at best, and arrogant at worst, to assume it is the broker of divine grace—the dispenser of charisms.

Surely one of the weightiest forms of human oppression, though rooted in the human condition rather than institutional law, is the experience of a marriage that has turned destructive. Defenders of obligatory celibacy remind the faithful of the shadow side of marriage—infidelity, abuse, deceit, divorce. The oppression of soul and spirit in a bad marriage is one of life's most painful tragedies. The harm that children suffer in these covenants of despair, beyond our means to measure, is horrific. Mandatory celibacy, the argument goes, spares priests from the ordeal of a marriage gone wrong. Still, for the priest without the charism for celibacy, the imposed condition remains oppressive. He may learn to live an authentic, integrated, emotionally healthy life as a celibate, but the imposed obligation restricts his freedom and oppresses his soul. It may appear that he has, over the years, personally and spiritually flourished as a celibate, but what is witnessed here is creative, often heroic, adjustment sustained by grace, ministry, good friends, and the discipline of prayer.

Just as it is possible for a prisoner to become liberated in spirit while behind bars, so it is possible for a priest to become fully human while living a celibate life, but in many cases it seems "to cost not less than everything."[4] And just as it is possible for a slave to know more true inner freedom than his master, it is possible for a priest to thrive spiritually and personally in the condition of mandated celibacy. But this does not justify the institution of celibacy any more than a personally liberated slave justifies the institution of slavery.

The degrees and levels of oppression, of course, are many and its scope broad. Daily we hear of economic oppression, political oppression, military oppression, religious oppression, gender and sexual oppression, class oppression, as well as other violations of human rights. Life, we know, is unfair. But oppression goes beyond claims of unfairness. It raises the spectrum of injustice. Is it fair to assert that mandatory celibacy as a manifestation of oppression is a violation of justice? The case has been made.

Consider Gary Wills critical analysis of Pope Paul VI's 1967 encyclical, *Priestly Celibacy*.[5] The encyclical builds on numerous citations from Scripture, but only two of the three New Testament citations dealing explicitly with celibacy are cited, not in the text of the document, but in a single footnote. Nor are these two passages quoted. They are simply cited. The non-quoted passages read, "A bishop must be irreproachable, the husband of only one wife . . ." (1 Tim 3:2), and "[a presbyter should be] a man unimpeachable, the husband of only one wife, with children of the faith . . ." (Titus 1: 7).

The third New Testament passage, the most germane to the justice issue, is overlooked completely. Neither cited nor quoted, it reads, "Have I [Paul] not the right [*exousia:* right, prerogative, power] to take a Christian wife about with me, like the rest of the apostles and the Lord's brothers, and Stone [Cephas]?" (1 Cor 9:5).[6] The "right" Paul claims but does not exercise is indeed claimed and exercised by Peter, the apostles, and the Lord's brothers—a right Latin rite diocesan priests have been denied since the twelfth century. When rights are restricted, limited, or denied without due cause, we are confronted with injustice.

In question here are the natural, human right to marry and the right of Christians to the sacraments. Of course, rights that are freely forgone, for example, Paul choosing not to exercise his prerogative to marry, may reflect the nobility of the human soul to place service of others ahead of the personal exercise of one's rights. On the other hand, when the forgoing of a right is linked to another good, especially the good inherent in priestly ministry to which one believes he is called, human freedom is attenuated. From this perspective, to require a priest to freely accept mandatory celibacy as part of the "priestly package" is specious. The controlling question should be: Does this candidate for priesthood give evidence not only of the charism of priestly ministry but also of the charism of celibacy?

Recognizing the problematic nature of trying to legislate a charism, some church authorities speak of mandated celibacy as a discipline—a noble discipline with roots traceable to the first centuries of the church. Arguing that mandated celibacy is primarily a discipline rather than a charism, however, is itself problematic. Can the discipline of celibacy take precedence over the sacrament of marriage? It has in the past, but should it in the future?

The church has and continues to legislate ascetical practices such as fasting and abstinence. But the essence of these mandated disciplines differs dramatically from the imposition of celibacy—ascetical practices remain extraneous to one's state in life while celibacy reaches to the core of one's existential experience of life. One finds a stronger argument in favor of mandating a discipline than a charism, but neither charisms nor ascetical practices should be subject to legislation.

If mandated celibacy is indeed a form of oppression for priests not enjoying the charism of celibacy, then what the hierarchic church has to say about oppression is relevant to our discussion. Following their 1971 World Synod held in Rome, the bishops published *Justice in the World.* Identifying with the oppressed of society, they observed, "We see the serious injustices that are building around the world of men [sic] a network of domination, oppression, and abuses which stifle freedom and keep the greater part of humanity from sharing in the building up and the enjoyment of a more just and more fraternal world." They go on to say, "In associations and among peoples themselves there emerges a new awareness shaking them out of fatalistic resignation and urging them to liberate themselves and become responsible for their destiny."[7] What keeps us from applying this prophetic message to certain conditions within the church?

Apparently many bishops and priests have done just that. Bishops' conferences from various parts of the world have called for the ordination of married men to meet the pastoral needs of their people. These bishops understand that forced fasting from the eucharist is itself a form of oppression and remaining silent in the face of such fasting a form of complicity in injustice. Priests themselves, in growing numbers, refuse to be resigned to the present burden of mandated celibacy and are calling upon their bishops for a review of the celibacy law—a review favored by most priests and an overwhelming majority of the laity.[8]

Certainly the dearth of priests and the pastoral needs of the people of God make the present situation urgent. At the beginning of the twenty-first century, there are more inactive priests in the U.S. than there are active diocesan priests—approximately twenty-two thousand inactive priests and twenty thousand active diocesan priests whose average age is over sixty. Many, if not most, of the inactive priests would be serving in our parishes if it were not for the law of celibacy. But even if our seminaries were full and our parishes adequately staffed, the issue of mandated celibacy would need to be addressed. It appears to growing numbers of clergy and laity to be in stark discord with the freedom of the gospel.

In March of 2000, preaching at the millennial Mass of repentance, Pope John Paul declared that "Christians have often denied the Gospel, yielding to a mentality of power."[9] Assuming the pope was not excluding Christians who are priests and bishops, curial officials, and other prelates of influence, the "yielding to a mentality of power" encompasses the hierarchic church as well as lay Christians. And where we find a mentality of power, the exercise of such power becomes quite soon oppressive.

Consider the oppressive force of mandated celibacy on women in the church. Celibate ecclesiastics, especially those wielding the greatest power, speak with unbridled confidence when insisting on the necessity of celibacy in the ranks of the clergy. In doing so they sustain a clerical culture which in turn creates an ethereal brotherhood that inevitably marginalizes women. It is in the "company of men" that the church's vision is articulated, its canons confirmed, its theology sanctioned, and its policies defended. All done with the supreme confidence that this is the state of affairs determined by the divine will.

A married diocesan clergy would not of itself restructure the life-stunting effects of the church's patriarchal society adapted from the Greco-Roman world, but it would surely soften its impact. At the present, the hierarchic church draws on the power of the feminine through its idealized and iconic devotion to the Virgin. What it desperately needs is the voice and influence of the feminine embodied in the lives of today's women of the church. A married clergy would bring us closer to that reality. It is reasonable to wonder if church authorities reacting to the clergy abuse scandals would have responded more pastorally and less corporately had they been parents and grandparents themselves, had they spouses with whom they might have pondered and fashioned a more Christlike outreach to victims and a more forthright resolve for the safety of children.

Mentalities of power, John Paul understood, are always and everywhere oppressive. Gospel power, on the other hand, is always and everywhere liberating—exercised for the pastoral care of the church and its mission to the world. Celibacy, I have argued here, is truly liberating for the individual who possesses the charism of celibate discipleship. And, as our experience confirms, it is blessing for the church. For the individual without the charism, however, mandated celibacy is anything but liberating. It is an unnecessary restriction and burden for thousands of priests and a source of suffering for the church itself.

The time is right. Catholics everywhere await the freeing of celibacy.

CHAPTER NINE

FREEING CELIBACY

Both Bishop Crowley and Monsignor Byrne, whom we met earlier, offer arresting examples of a providential design at work in mandated celibacy. Are these two men, representative of countless celibate priests who have found deep joy in their priesthood, recipients of the charism of celibacy? Or, responding to the mystery of grace in their lives, were they able to draw on their souls' urgent promptings to forge meaningful, intimate, celibate friendships in the face of social and ecclesial pressures to forgo such relationships and, thus, make celibacy "work" for them? Are they *de facto* celibates (effectively living mandated celibacy) or *de jure* celibates (responding to the pull of charismatic celibacy)? Most would confess, I believe, that whatever the answer, they have sensed the mystery of grace in their lives—a providential design.

Without question, the witness of celibate friendship is counter-cultural to the indulgence and radical individualism typical of Western society. We rightly celebrate the example of deep, intimate, chaste friendships marking the Catholic spiritual heritage—friendships such as Francis and Clare, Jordan and Diana, and John Henry Newman and his close friend, Ambrose St. John, with whom Newman is buried.[1] These graced relationships remind us that there is rich, human fulfillment possible without marriage. The presumption holds, however, that these notable friendships were shared by charismatic celibates, men and women who experienced celibacy as their truth.

Priests without the charism of celibacy, if they have adjusted to the obligation without losing their basic integrity and humanity, are for the most part men who have achieved and nurtured profound, intimate, and chaste friendships with women (in the case of straight priests) and men (in the case of gay priests). The stories of these friendships tend to remain untold and uncelebrated since they often meet with skepticism and even cynicism when they do become known.

In spite of the providential design that can be discerned in the lives of many priests, these deep and abiding friendships should not be read as a divine endorsement of obligatory celibacy. Because God can bring good out of any human circumstance, any human institution, any human suffering, does not mean that God wills, indeed blesses, the circumstance, the institution, the suffering.

Charismatic celibacy will remain a great gift to the church. Mandated celibacy awaits repeal.

Charisms, in many cases, defy easy identification in a given individual. Some monks and nuns clearly manifest the charism for vowed religious life. In their hearts, they know that monastic, community life is their truth. Others, often after many years in community, come to see that it is not their gift. Moreover, charismatic celibacy, unlike, say, the charism of preaching (we know it when we hear it), sits side by side—often amidst considerable tension—with human sexual longing in the deepest chambers of the human soul, both drawing energy from the same divine spark. Some days, celibates may think they do indeed possess the charism. Other days they are not so sure. Once, sitting with a wise, retired priest in his nineties, I asked him what he thought of celibacy. "Celibacy is okay," he responded wryly, "during the day!" He would agree, I believe, that discerning the reality of the charism requires a life of prayer, wise spiritual direction, good and trustworthy friends, and a faith community willing to be radically honest with the individual pondering a life of celibate chastity.

Perhaps the charism of celibacy is much like humility. We are instinctively wary of anyone who claims it. What we do know about celibacy is that it is a rare charism bestowed upon relatively few men and women. We also know that it is a demanding gift, sustained by evident psychosexual maturity, true friendships, and a rich interior life of faith and prayer.

Recall the canonical foundation for mandated celibacy: *Clerics are obliged to observe perfect and perpetual continence for the sake of the kingdom of heaven and therefore are obliged to observe celibacy, which is a special gift of God, by which sacred ministers can adhere more easily to Christ with an undivided heart and can more freely dedicate themselves to the service of God and humankind.*

Two obligations are stressed: the obligation to *continence* and the obligation to *celibacy*. Where do these obligations come from? Not from Christ, nor from the gospel. The first obligation to a life of sexual continence is an assertion of the hierarchic church—for the Latin rite only.

"For the sake of the kingdom of heaven" is left hanging. What precisely is meant when church authorities say a Latin rite priest must be continent for the sake of the kingdom of heaven? Is this declaration drawn out of thin air? Is it simply an appeal to the tradition of the last nine centuries of church history? Does it not reveal an outdated, dualistic theological anthropology?

Further questions come to mind. Are not married priests of the Eastern rites married for the sake of the kingdom? Are not married Orthodox priests married for the sake of the kingdom of heaven? Are the hundreds of married Latin rite priests (converts with special dispensations from celibacy) less committed to the kingdom? Is there not an implicit assertion here that married priests are less committed to the kingdom of heaven? Moreover, are not all sacramental marriages oriented to the kingdom of heaven? Finally, are not all Christians, because of their baptismal dignity, committed to the kingdom of heaven?

The deduction that follows the obligation to continence in canon 277 is puzzling. We find ourselves faced with a *therefore* that rests solely on an assertion that is without support from the gospel nor from the tradition of the first millennium of the church's history. *[T]herefore, [clerics] are obliged to observe celibacy, which is a special gift of God. . . .* Obligatory celibacy, it appears, is essentially a canonical edifice. The walls of this edifice consist of two non-biblical assertions with the kingdom of heaven as its vaulted ceiling—all loosely tethered with a weak "therefore."

A special gift? Yes, indeed. But how do church authorities know to whom this special gift has been bestowed? It appears presumptuous of church officials to declare that they know this special gift will be bestowed on candidates for the Latin priesthood but not on candidates for the Eastern rite priesthood; that while this special gift was apparently not widely bestowed for well beyond the first millennium of the church, it was indeed bestowed on Latin rite candidates from the middle of the twelfth century on.

Canon 277 continues, . . . *by which sacred ministers can adhere more easily to Christ with an undivided heart and can more freely dedicate themselves to the service of God and humankind.* How do church officials know this? Have bishops asked their priests to speak from their celibate experience about their ability to adhere more easily to Christ? Are celibate priests really freer to dedicate themselves to the service of God and humankind? Are their hearts really more undivided than the hearts of their brother priests who are married? Perhaps some bishops have asked but most have not. Sociologists and psychologists and writers ask about priests' experiences of celibacy, but bishops do not. They really don't want to know.

Celibacy, I have come to see, remains a neuralgic issue because it has come to be linked to the ideal of radical fidelity to the gospel. There is a common drive within the committed Christian that seeks to shape his or her life in such a way that gospel values are manifest. In the second and third centuries Christians bore heroic and ideal witness to their faith in Christ by their steadfast perseverance in the face of persecution that often led to martyrdom. Once the bloody persecution of Christians came to an end around the beginning of the fourth century, many Christians looked for another way to radically and ideally live the gospel.

Soon the "white martyrdom" of celibacy became the badge of radical commitment to Christ and his teaching. The celibacy of the early church fathers and the celibacy of monks and nuns came to be acknowledged as the ideal and radical path of gospel discipleship. Where the sparks of idealism erupted into flame in the hearts of many disciples, the turn to a celibate way of life inevitably followed. In spite of the church's long history of married priests, bishops, and popes, the forgoing of the right to marry came to be associated with the radical disciple, the "true believer."

So, it is not surprising that large numbers of seminarians, priests, and laity still associate celibacy with radical fidelity to the gospel. One seminarian put it this way: "The young men who are serious enough about their faith to feel a call to the priesthood are not the kind of men for whom celibacy is an insurmountable obstacle. Those truly called are by definition those who are ready to accept the grace of God by which the impossible becomes possible. We want to witness to the world the Good News of salvation, and to do this we must be radical—we must be set apart. And what is more radical in today's world than to accept freely the charism of celibacy?"[2] Note the assumption that the charism of celibacy has been offered to the seminarian.

This kind of desire to be a radical witness to the world of the Good News of salvation is grounded in an idealism that deserves support and encouragement. But, a problematic theology is at work here. The issue is not whether obligatory celibacy is an insurmountable obstacle, it clearly is not; but whether it is a necessary obligation, a necessary obstacle. Our brief review of the history of celibacy shows that it is not. The point is made that if one feels called to the priesthood one should be ready to accept the grace of God "by which the impossible becomes possible." We are back to the traditional argument for mandatory celibacy. *Accept the obligation of celibacy and you will be given the grace to live a faithful celibate life.* This is so, it appears, because the church insists it is so. From this perspective, one need not struggle to discern the charism of celibacy because the candidate for the Latin rite priesthood will be given the grace to achieve "the impossible." In fact, the seminarian but needs to "accept freely the charism of celibacy." Gifts, however, must first be offered before they can be received. It remains presumptive to argue that God will give the charism of celibacy to every seminarian who feels called to priesthood. It would seem that God has not done so in the past and that God continues to call men to the priesthood and to marriage in the Eastern rite Catholic churches and in the Orthodox Church.

Neither the New Testament nor the first millennium of the church identifies radical fidelity to the gospel with celibacy. For individuals who have received the gift of celibacy, a celibate life well lived is indeed a powerful, radical witness to the gospel. But obligatory celibacy continues to be held in the minds of many as *the* paradigm of radical discipleship. The theological support for such an ideal, it should be clear, is built on a biblical foundation that is both meager and precariously employed.

Radical commitment to Christ and his gospel remains the challenge of all who are baptized into the communion of the church. Priests, both married and celibate, are called as leaders and servants of God's people to bear witness, by the grace of God, in and through their preaching and spiritual leadership. With their brothers and sisters in faith, they bear witness in accord with the charisms and ministries entrusted to them.

Witness to the gospel, of course, abounds. Consider the witness of what we might call "circumstantial celibates"— those countless men and women living alone without the support of a religious community and without the apparent charism of celibacy. For many widows, widowers, divorced, and separated, bravely bearing the everyday ache of loneliness and loss is a witness to the gospel. Consider, too, the untold numbers of individuals who would like to marry only to have their desire and hope go unfulfilled. Their faithful lives bear witness. So do parents struggling to raise children in their Christian faith. So do the many thousands of college graduates who give a year or more of their lives to one of the service programs sponsored by church and government agencies. And so do people who courageously suffer illness, hardship, and oppression. In the midst of the storms of life and the unimaginable violence of our times, we see the light of Christ in the eyes of ordinary people bearing radical witness to the gospel.

We should be wary of any seminarian, priest, or bishop who isn't eager to bear radical witness to the gospel. But if that radical witness isn't essentially linked to celibacy, where and how is it manifested? For one called to priesthood, grace builds on the aptitude for spiritual leadership—an ability to preach the word, to champion the poor and exploited, to care for the pastoral needs of those who receive him as their priest. Such a life of preaching and ministry is indeed a radical witness.

Let the clergy, as the pastoral leaders of the church, live the beatitudes, care for the least among them, preach the liberating word of God, embrace the humility of their ancestors in the communion of saints, and live as the least of Christ's disciples. In a word—let them strive to live a life of *gospel simplicity*. To the extent priests and bishops embraced simplicity of life, poverty of spirit, and humility of heart, clericalism would be dissolved, their integrity restored, and their credibility reclaimed. This, indeed, would be a radical witness—something worthy of any seminarian's idealism.

Living simply and humbly by the lights of the gospel in a culture saturated with self-serving ambition and insatiable material lust is indeed counter-cultural—and radical. Priests and bishops, as members of the faithful, stand under the judgment of the gospel they preach. And it is the implicit judgment of this radical gospel that keeps them in a state of *holy anxiety*. Do their patterns of living and interacting echo the word of liberation and deliverance they proclaim? Can any of them answer with an unequivocal yes?

No longer does the priest's celibate status signal ideal, radical commitment to the people of God—neither do clerical clothes nor ecclesiastical titles. Today's Catholics, disillusioned by the betrayals of bishops and priests, the scandals of sexual abuse and financial impropriety, see right through *external* signs of radical, ideal commitment. What they desire is true spiritual leadership; what they hunger and thirst for is inspired preaching and solid spiritual guidance. When they see these traits in the person of their pastor, whether the priest is married or celibate matters little. Authenticity and credibility, Catholics now understand, are determined neither by the celibate state nor ordination in and of themselves. They are matters of the heart. And at the heart of the matter is the minister's ability to witness to the hope against hope that Christ is our all and his gospel our path to new life.

Let me conclude on a personal note. I'm now in my fifth decade as a priest and words cannot express my gratitude for the privilege of preaching this radical gospel I so feebly attempt to live. Gospel simplicity?—I'm not sure I know the least thing about it. But I am convinced that the gospel's radical invitation to a new way of life is the source of our salvation and liberation. To the extent there has been some radical witness to my life, I would hope that it has been the semblance of gospel fidelity that has emerged from time to time. On the other hand, I'm not at all sure of the witness value of my celibate state. It no doubt has earned the respect of some, perhaps many. But it is not at all the heart of the matter.

Celibacy, it must be conceded, has been the defining mark, the *signature* of ordination for the past nine centuries. As such it has been engraved in the Catholic collective unconscious—where it has rested more or less uncontested for almost a millennium. But no longer. Both laity and clergy now see that the *law* of celibacy is, at best, counterproductive for the life and mission of the church. Priesthood's true signature is *spiritual leadership* grounded in the defining mark of every Christian who takes his or her discipleship seriously—fidelity to the God we cannot see, to gospel simplicity writ large as is fitting for spiritual leaders and preachers. What St. Paul said to the Philippians, the people of God now say to their priests, "Conduct yourselves in a way worthy of the gospel of Christ."[3] This, it would seem, is quite enough.

Charismatic celibacy, I have argued here, is indeed a blessing for the church. As a freely bestowed gift of the Spirit, it deserves to be released from canonical mandate as a condition for ordination. The time has come to set celibacy free.

NOTES

Chapter One: The Mystique of Celibacy

1. In addition to Deborah Kerr in *Heaven Knows Mr. Allison* (1957), actresses capturing the mystique of celibacy include Jennifer Jones in *The Song of Bernadette* (1943), Ingrid Berman in *The Bells of St. Mary's* (1945), and Audrey Hepburn in *The Nun's Story* (1959).

2. Augustine, *Confessions* 2:3; *On Marriage and Concupiscence* 1:16.

3. Paul Tillich, *The Interpretation of History* (New York: Charles Scribner's Sons, 1936) 80–81, and Rollo May, *Love and Will* (New York: W. W. Norton & Company, 1969). "The daimonic is any natural function which has the power to take over the whole person. Sex and eros, anger and rage, and the craving for power are examples. The daimonic can be either creative or destructive and is normally both." 123.

4. See Mark Jordan, *The Silence of Sodom: Homosexuality in Modern Catholicism* (The University of Chicago Press, 2000) 181–182, and Ellis Hanson, *Decadence and Catholicism* (Cambridge, MA: Harvard University Press, 1997) 241–263.

5. Ronald Rolheiser, *The Holy Longing* (New York: Doubleday, 1999). "To sleep alone is to be poor. . . . To sleep alone is to be outside the norm for human intimacy and to acutely feel the sting of that." 210.

Chapter Two: Celibacy as Charism

1. "I believe God made me for a purpose, but he also made me fast. And when I run I feel his pleasure." Eric Liddell played by Ian Charleson in the 1981 film, *Chariots of Fire*.

2. A beer advertisement in the June 2005 *Vogue* magazine proposed carrying a membership card that reads, "Celibacy United, Member in Good Standing." Beneath the signature line was the following: "I pledge to remain celibate for the rest of my life, content with the joy of good friends and fine conversation." The ad's copy: "Can we make your night out better? Sure. If the guys don't see that you want to be left alone, let them see this (the clipped out membership card). It'll douse their flame real fast. In fact, the only thing colder is that Bud Light in front of you." Both clever and cynical, the ad is nevertheless telling. Freed from the undercurrent of sexual politics, celibate friends make for good company. They are no strangers to "the joy of good friends and fine conversation."

3. John Crowley, "The Gift of Married Priests," *The Tablet,* July 2, 2005.

4. Paul Elie, *The Life You Save May Be Your Own* (New York: Farrar, Straus and Giroux, 2003) 444.

Chapter Three: Celibacy as Obligation

1. For an argument proposing that celibacy is inherent to the priesthood and that married priests are to practice continence, see Christian Cochini, *The Apostolic Origins of Priestly Celibacy* (San Francisco: Ignatius Press, 1990).

2. Until 1929, Eastern rite priests in the United States and Canada were permitted to marry before ordination. But at the urging of some U.S. bishops, the freedom of these priests to marry was curtailed for fear that Latin rite priests, envious of their Eastern rite brothers, would desire the same freedom.

3. Why, it is reasonable to ask, hasn't the church made public the number of married Latin rite priests?

4. It appears the vast majority of these clergy were prompted to leave their own communion because of the ordination of women.

5. John Paul II, Apostolic Exhortation, *Familiaris Consortio* (November 22, 1981) 16: *AAS* 74 (1982) 98.

6. John Paul II, Apostolic Exhortation, *I Will Give You Shepherds* [*Pastores Dabo Vobis*] (March 25, 1992) 29.

7. Ibid.

8. See Richard McBrien, *The Lives of the Popes* (San Francisco: HarperCollins, 1997).

9. See Eugene Kennedy and Victor Heckler, *The Catholic Priest in the United States: Psychological Investigations* (Washington, D.C.: United States Catholic Conference, 1971), and Andrew Greeley, *The Catholic Priest in the United States: Sociological Investigations* (Washington, D.C.: United States Catholic Conference, 1972).

10. See Louis Bouyer, *The Church of God* (Chicago: Franciscan Herald Press, 1982) chapter 3.

11. Recently installed bishops in New York and Illinois encountered strong criticism from their priests and people when large amounts of money were spent or claimed for enhancing their episcopal residences.

12. See William E. Phipps, *Clerical Celibacy: The Heritage* (New York: Continuum, 2004) especially chapters 2, 4, and 5.

13. John Paul II, *The Theology of Marriage and Celibacy* (Boston: Daughters of St. Paul, 1986) 90, 102.

14. Cicero writes that the "most sacred of priestly offices" was that of the vestal virgins. Cicero, *De domo suo*, 53, 136.

15. John Crowley, *The Tablet*, July 2, 2005.

Chapter Four: Celibacy's Exceptions

1. Interestingly, John Paul II, in his apostolic exhortation, *I Will Give You Shepherds*, encourages seminary personnel to hold nothing back from seminarians relating to the realities of priestly life.

2. *The Changing Face of the Priesthood* is fundamentally about integrity, personal and institutional integrity. My book, *Sacred Silence*, addressed the dynamic of denial at work in the hierarchic church.

3. Richard Schoenherr, *Goodbye Father* (New York: Oxford, 2002) 112, 176. See also Dean Hoge, *The First Five Years of the Priesthood* (Collegeville, MN: Liturgical Press, 2002) 60–64, and Dean Hoge and Jaqueline Wenger, *Evolving Visions of the Priesthood* (Collegeville, MN: Liturgical Press, 2004).

4. John Paul II, *To All Pastors* (1992) 29, and "Church Committed to Priestly Celibacy," *L'Osservatore Romano*, July 21, 1993.

5. John Paul II, "The Apostolic Exhortation on the Family," *Origins*, December 24, 1981, 443.

6. The six main Eastern rites in the U. S. are the Chaldean, Syrian, Maronite, Coptic, Armenian, and Byzantine.

7. "Decree on Eastern Catholic Churches," *The Documents of Vatican II* (New York: The America Press, 1966).

8. William Phipps, *Clerical Celibacy: The Heritage* (New York: Continuum, 2004) 121ff.

9. Michael Crosby, *Celibacy: Means of Control or Mandate of the Heart?* (Notre Dame, IN: Ave Maria Press, 1996) 79.

10. It is said that in Germany, everything is forbidden unless permitted; in Italy, everything is permitted unless forbidden; and in Russia, everything is forbidden, even what is permitted.

Chapter Five: Celibacy's Shadow

1. See Michael Papish, *Clericalism* (Collegeville, MN: Liturgical Press, 2003), and Donald Cozzens, *Sacred Silence: Denial and the Crisis in the Church* (Collegeville, MN: Liturgical Press, 2002, 2004) 112–123.

2. Jane Anderson, *Priests in Love: Roman Catholic Clergy and Their Intimate Friendships* (New York: Continuum, 2005).

3. The National Review Board Report issued on February 27, 2004.

4. Richard P. McBrien, *Lives of the Popes* (San Francisco: Harper-Collins, 1997) 267.

Chapter Six: Celibacy and Homosexuality

1. Donald Cozzens, *The Changing Face of the Priesthood* (Collegeville, MN, Liturgical Press, 2000) chapter 7, "Considering Orientation," 97–110.

2. Richard P. McBrien, "Homosexuality and the Priesthood: Questions We Can't Keep in the Closet," *Commonweal* (June 19, 1987) 380–383, and Andrew M. Greeley, "Bishops Paralyzed over Heavily Gay Priesthood," *National Catholic Reporter,* November 10, 1989, 13–14.

3. Donald Cozzens, *The Changing Face of the Priesthood* and *Sacred Silence: Denial and the Crisis in the Church* (Collegeville, MN: Liturgical Press, 2002).

4. "Instruction Concerning the Criteria for the Discernment of Vocations with Regards to Persons with Homosexual Tendencies in View of Their Admission to the Seminary and to Holy Orders." Congregation for Catholic Education, November 4, 2005. The cover letter to bishops accompanying the Instruction further directed bishops not to appoint men with homosexual tendencies to be rectors or to serve on seminary faculties.

5. *America,* September 30, 2002, 8–9.

6. Ellis Hanson, *Decadence and Catholicism* (Cambridge, MA: Harvard University Press, 1997) 7.

7. Ibid., 297.

8. *The Changing Face of the Priesthood,* chapter 3, "Loving as a Celibate," 25–43.

9. Ibid., 43.

Chapter Seven: Celibacy as Power

1. Boniface VIII, *Unam Sanctam,* 1302: "We declare, affirm, and define as a truth necessary for salvation that every human being is subject to the Roman pontiff."

2. Donald Cozzens, *The Changing Face of the Priesthood,* chapters 4, "Facing the Unconscious," and 5, "Becoming a Man."

3. Alexander Schmemann, *The Journals of Alexander Schmemann,* (New York: St. Vladimir's Seminary Press, 2000).

4. Harry J. Byrne, "One Man's Vocation," *Commonweal,* July 16, 2004, 15.

Chapter Eight: Celibacy as Oppression

1. Michael Crosby, *Celibacy: Means of Control or Mandate of the Heart* (Notre Dame: Ave Maria Press, 1996). Crosby tells of a brother Franciscan who felt as oppressed by celibacy as a diocesan priest might. "I wanted to be a priest. I wanted to minister as a priest. The Franciscans were the only priests I knew when I was growing up. So I entered them. I ended up being a Franciscan because it was all part of the package." 63.

2. See Tim Unsworth, *The Last Priests in America* (New York: Crossroad, 1991), and Jane Anderson, *Priests in Love* (New York: Continuum, 2005), for numerous examples of men blessed with the charism of priesthood but not the charism of celibacy.

3. Some Protestant denominations have made marriage compulsory for their ministers. See William Phipps, *Clerical Celibacy: The Heritage* (New York: Continuum, 2004) 74.

4. John Crowley, *The Tablet*, July 2, 2005.

5. Gary Wills, *Papal Sin: Structures of Deceit* (New York: Doubleday, 2000) chapter 8, "The Pope's Eunuchs," 124–125.

6. The passages quoted here are from the New English Bible.

7. Quoted in David O'Brien et al., eds., *Catholic Social Thought: The Documentary Heritage* (Maryknoll, NY: Orbis Books, 1992) 288–289.

8. William V. D'Antonio, James D. Davidson, Dean R. Hoge, and Katherine Meyer, *American Catholics: Gender, Generation, and Commitment* (New York: Altamira Press, 2001). See also Christine Schenk, "Celibates on Celibacy," *Commonweal*, November 19, 2004, 24, and the *National Catholic Reporter*, September 30, 2005, special research supplement.

9. John Paul II, "Universal Prayer: Confession of Sins and Asking for Forgiveness," March 12, 2000, www.jcrelations.net/stimnts/vatican3-00.htm.

Chapter Nine: Freeing Celibacy

1. John Henry Newman, *Apologia*, 1864, in www.Newmanreader.org. Newman writes of his friend: "And to you especially, dear Ambrose St. John; whom God gave me, when He took every one else away; who are the link between my old life and my new; who have now for twenty-one years been so devoted to me, so patient, so zealous, so tender; who have let me lean so hard upon you; who have watched me so narrowly; who have never thought of yourself, if I was in question."

2. Franz Klein, "John Paul II Priests," *Commonweal*, August 12, 2005, 25.

3. Philippians 1:27a (New American Bible).

SELECT BIBLIOGRAPHY

Alison, James. *Faith Beyond Resentment: Fragments Catholic and Gay*. New York: Crossroad, 2001.

Anderson, Jane. *Priests in Love: Roman Catholic Clergy and Their Intimate Relationships*. New York: Continuum, 2005.

Boswell, John. *Christianity, Social Tolerance, and Homosexuality*. The University of Chicago Press, 1980.

Carroll, James. *Toward a New Catholic Church*. Boston: Houghton Mifflin, 2002.

Cornwell, John. *Breaking Faith*. New York: Viking, 2001.

Cozzens, Donald. *The Changing Face of the Priesthood*. Collegeville, MN: Liturgical Press, 2000.

————. *Sacred Silence: Denial and the Crisis in the Church*. Collegeville, MN: Liturgical Press, 2002.

————. *Faith That Dares to Speak*. Collegeville, MN: Liturgical Press, 2004.

Crosby, Michael. *Celibacy: Means of Control or Mandate of the Heart*. Notre Dame, IN: Ave Maria Press, 1996.

Dinter, Paul. *The Other Side of the Altar*. New York: Farrar, Straus, & Giroux, 2003.

Doyle, Thomas P., A. W. R. Sipe, Patrick J. Wall. *Sex, Priests, and Secret Codes*. Los Angeles, CA: Volt Press, 2006.

Flannery, Tony. *From the Inside: A Priest's View of the Catholic Church*. Dublin, Ireland: Mercier Press, 1999.

Fox, Thomas. *Sexuality and Catholicism*. New York: Braziller, 1995.

Gibson, David. *The Coming Catholic Church*. San Francisco: Harper, 2003.

Goergen, Donald, and Ann Garrido, eds. *The Theology of the Priesthood*. Collegeville, MN: Michael Glazer, 2000.

Hanson, Ellis. *Decadence and Catholicism*. Cambridge, MA: Harvard University Press, 1997.

Heaps, John. *A Love That Dares to Question: A Bishop Challenges His Church*. Grand Rapids, MI: William B. Eerdmans, 1998.

Hedin, Raymond. *Married to the Church*. Bloomington & Indianapolis: Indiana University Press, 1995.

Hoge, Dean. *The First Five Years of the Priesthood*. Collegeville, MN: Liturgical Press, 2002.

Hoge, Dean, and Jacqueline Wenger. *Evolving Visions of the Priesthood*. Collegeville, MN: Liturgical Press, 2003.

Jordan, Mark D. *The Silence of Sodom: Homosexuality in Modern Catholicism*. University of Chicago Press, 2000.

Kelly, John. *The Oxford Dictionary of Popes*. New York: Oxford, 1986.

Kennedy, Eugene C. *The Unhealed Wound: The Church and Human Sexuality*. New York: St. Martin's Griffin, 2001.

McBrien, Richard P. *Lives of the Popes*. HarperSanFrancisco, 1997.

Morris, Charles. *American Catholic: The Saints and Sinners Who Built America's Most Powerful Church*. New York: Random House, Vintage, 1998.

Murphy, Sheila. *The Delicate Dance*. New York: Crossroad, 1992.

Phipps, William E. *Clerical Celibacy: The Heritage*. New York: Continuum, 2004.

Ranke-Heinemann, Uta. *Eunuchs for the Kingdom of Heaven*. New York: Doubleday, 1990.

Rice, David. *Shattered Vows*. New York: Morrow, 1990.

Schoenherr, Richard A., Lawrence A. Young, and Tsan-Yuang Cheng. *Full Pews and Empty Altars: Demographics of the Priest Shortage in the United States Catholic Dioceses*. Madison: University of Wisconsin Press, 1993.

Schoenherr, Richard A., edited with an introduction by David Yamane. *Goodbye Father: The Celibate Male Priesthood and the Future of the Catholic Church.* New York: Oxford University Press, 2002.

Sipe, Richard. *Celibacy in Crisis.* New York: Brunner, 2003.

Steinfels, Peter. *A People Adrift.* New York: Simon & Schuster, 2003.

Wills, Gary. *Papal Sin: Structures of Deceit.* New York: Doubleday, 2000.